THE THINGS LEFT UNSAID

ANNELL ST. CHARLES

For Permission requests, write to:
YBR Publishing, LLC
PO Box 4904
Beaufort SC 29903-4904
contact@ybrpub.com
843-597-0912

THE THINGS LEFT UNSAID

ANNELL ST. CHARLES

ISBN-13: 978-1-7339992-5-0
ISBN 10 – 1-7339992-5-0

Cover design by Jack Gannon & Cyndi Williams-Barnier

Bill Barnier – Senior Editor, YBR Publishing
Cyndi Williams-Barnier – Production Editor, YBR Publishing
Jack Gannon- Production Manager, YBR Publishing

THE THINGS LEFT UNSAID

DEDICATION

For my husband, Constantine (Costas) Tsinakis, who has never failed to boost my confidence, regardless of how great or small the dream I choose to pursue.

ACKNOWLEDGEMENTS

There are several people to whom I would like to offer my deep appreciation for their assistance and support in helping me turn the idea of this book into a reality. My husband, Costas Tsinakis, for being the first person to read my initial draft, provide constructive advice, and assist me with the formatting of the final manuscript. John Tutterow and Susan Schipani, who were also first draft readers, and who provided valuable comments and advice. Judy Therber, whose grammar and punctuation suggestions were most helpful. All of the members of my Nashville "Book and Wine Club", who influenced my work by allowing me to hear what they had to say about numerous books over the last 20+ years. Jerry Park, for sharing his experience and advice about the indie publishing process. Tish Owen and Jane Bradley, whose courage at putting their own words into print inspired me when my own self-confidence was lagging. The members of YBR Publishing (Bill Barnier, Cyndi Williams-Barnier, Jack Gannon) for their help on re-editing and releasing this second edition. Finally, my daughter and son, Sophia and Andreas Tsinakis, thank you for your enduring love.

"The bitterest tears shed over graves are for words left unsaid and deeds left undone."

~Harriet Beecher Stowe

THE THINGS LEFT UNSAID

Chapter 1

I grew up in a quiet house. It's not that it was totally absent of noise. It just wasn't full of the kind of vibrant and cheery sounds I imagined other people would describe as customary in their homes. My father was a man of few words, at least when it came to communicating with his family. His silence was the loudest thing about him, and I tended to shy away from him in fear I would become the unwilling target of his stern reserve. My mother rarely spoke either, unless it was to voice the silent reprimands of my father; despite the fact that adults had a favorite saying in those days "that children should be seen and not heard". I felt it was in my best interest to be neither. So, I became a shadow child, only leaving the faintest impression of my existence as I passed silently through their world.

By the time I entered elementary school, I had become quite adept at entertaining myself with endless hours of imaginary adventures with playmates who existed only in my mind. My teachers interpreted my silence as shyness, and set about trying to *bring me out of my shell* by calling on me to speak out in class with regular frequency. The idea of expressing my thoughts out loud was terrifying, and I responded by sinking deeper into my silence. My classmates regarded my remoteness as an indication that I was different. "Weird" was one of their kinder words for how they viewed me. Eventually, the teachers decided I must have special needs, which would be best nurtured in a controlled environment. At least that's the explanation they gave to my parents. In truth, I suspected they just wanted a way to get me out of their hair so they could devote their time to children who were easier to deal with. Since this was the 1960s, and a time well before the days of actual special education classrooms, those children who were deemed different were sent to the school cafeteria for "private instruction". They were given an assignment, then left alone to figure it out for themselves. Since the group consisted of a mismatched bunch ranging from the really shy to the terribly scary, there was very little learning that actually took place. My way of dealing with this was to seek out the farthest corner of the room and bury my head in my books, hoping not to draw any attention to myself. It usually worked.

It's very likely I would have continued to drift into a never-ending spiral of withdrawal had it not been for one amazing teacher. Mrs. Gaddis was one of the school's first-grade teachers who was known for her passionate forays into all things English. English instruction, that is. One day, as she was passing through the cafeteria during one of our private instruction periods, she wandered over to see what we were up to. Once she realized what was really happening, she volunteered to spend her free period attempting to actually give us some real educational instruction. Eventually, the principal decided to formally assign her to the *special* students when a few parents got wind of what was happening and started raising a small ruckus. I figured she had been assigned responsibility for us because there was no money in the system to hire anyone out-right, and no one else wanted the job. I never knew whether she regarded her extra assignment as a burden or a gift, but she always managed to make those of us who found ourselves under her tutelage feel only the *special* part of our label. Under her gentle guidance and kind encouragement, I began to realize the voices in my head gained magical qualities when I allowed them to be heard by someone else.

By the time I reached high school, I had become rather adept at verbal expression. Yet, there was still something deep inside of me that held me back from truly saying what I felt. By then, I had begun to write poems as a means of self-expression. A poem, I felt, was like an abstract painting; interpreted and experienced differently by all who viewed it. I was comforted by the awareness that if one of my poems were to offend, the offense could be explained away by an error of interpretation.

Over time, as I gained confidence, I began to venture beyond poetry to writing about the real and often mundane details of daily life. In an uncharacteristically brave move, I signed up to join the staff of my high school newspaper. Journalism, I soon discovered, provided me with an avenue of expression that was unmatched in any other form of writing. It was a way of speaking the truth, but in a voice that was impersonal and safe, or, at least I imagined that to be the case. The beauty of inexperience is that ignorance truly can be blissful.

During my sophomore year, my job was to produce feature stories for our school paper, *The Bernard Banner*, on the fascinating activities of my classmates. I grew tired of spelling contests, school dances, and volunteer trips to Haiti. A busload of teenagers would engage in unbridled alcohol consumption and late-night antics under the guise of building international relations. It seemed the only relations they were interested in building were among themselves. But, of course, I couldn't report on that.

In my junior year, I decided to venture outside the walls of my school to see what the rest of the world was doing that might be worth writing about. It was Grammy time in Nashville, when local and national music artists were vying for the coveted symbol of their musical prowess. John Hartford was up for a Grammy that year for his song *Gentle on My Mind*, and somehow, I got the idea that I should cover that story. Through some remarkable accident of good fortune and detective work, I managed to score an

13

interview with Mr. Hartford, which was published in my school newspaper. When his song won a Grammy, news spread of the high school student who had scooped the story out of the hands of the local journalists. I was shocked by the accolades that my feat drew, and more than a little uncomfortable with the attention it brought. Yet at the same time, I felt a level of exhilaration I had never experienced before. Writing became my voice, and I felt like I was finally being heard.

My journalism teacher, Miss DeBose, reacted to the news by promoting me to Editor for my senior year, a move that ended up being my worst nightmare. It was the Peter Principle for a writer; take someone out of doing what they do well, and give them a job they are neither qualified for nor interested in doing. It was a guaranteed recipe for failure. "Georgia, sometimes in life we have to do what we should instead of what we want." I stood a good six inches in height over Miss DeBose, but she commandeered her five feet like a small tank loaded with explosives. The one thing we all knew about Miss DeBose was that you didn't cross her. So, I became the editor of *The Bernard Banner.*

As I could have predicted, I bombed as an editor, mainly because one of the chief jobs was to write editorials. Editorials required you to have an opinion. I had lots of opinions, but none I felt brave enough to put into writing. Luckily, one of the feature writers was great at writing editorials, but bad at coming up with feature stories. So, we secretly switched. I have no doubt Miss DeBose knew what we were up to, but there was no way she was going to expose her mistake by confronting us. I'm not sure if our switch had any bearing on what happened next. I ended up being offered a job right out of high school on one of our two local newspapers.

At that time, Nashville supported two newspapers – *The Nashville News*, which came out in the morning, and its rival, *The Daily Courier* that followed up with an evening addition of the local and national news. I was offered a chance to work for the *News.*

Despite the advice of my teachers, I decided to forego my plans for college and jump right into my journalistic career. My parents didn't object to my choice. In fact, they didn't take much notice of what my plans might be. They seemed to be relieved that I would be paying my own way in the world sooner rather than later, and I was truthfully relieved at the chance to break free of the stifling existence of their home. Years later, when I had the opportunity to explore my early years and try to decipher what made my parents tick, I could only come up the explanation that they were locked in their own misery. I never came close to figuring out what made them that way, since I never managed to find a way to speak to them about it. But I was eventually able to come to the awareness that how they were had very little, if anything, to do with me. While that realization freed me from some of the self-blame, I cloaked myself with guilt during the first couple of decades of my life; it didn't really "make it all better". Nothing can do that for a child, except the accumulation of time and a boatload of counseling.

As it turned out, my decision to take the job at the *News* ended up being a less than stellar move. In my inexperience, I failed to ask exactly what job I was being offered. I envisioned myself cruising around Nashville, taking in local events, hobnobbing with celebrities and prominent locals, and producing stories that would garner me a shower of praise from anyone who read one of my pieces. Instead, my job title was *copy girl*, which really meant glorified *gopher*. My days were spent getting the mail bags from the local post office, picking up coffee and pastries for the early morning city desk crew, changing ribbons on typewriters and news service machines, sharpening pencils, and fetching more coffee from the vending machine down the hall. In between all of that, I ran copy back and forth between my more seasoned co-workers who took pleasure that the greenhorn was taken down a notch or two from the high-horse she road in on. My daily life fell into a steady, unexciting routine.

Chapter 2

It was three years before I was finally given my first writing assignment for *The Nashville News*. One of the problems was my age. I was barely eighteen when I came to work for the paper. At twenty-one, I was still the baby of the group. That I looked even younger than my age did nothing to enhance my credibility. The bigger problem though was my gender. The newspaper business was then and, to some extent, still is, a *good-old-boys club*, especially in the South. It was okay for a female to fetch their coffee and donuts and listen to their trumped-up accounts of reporting adventures. But suggest she might have ideas of her own worthy of printing and you may as well have suggested *Jack Daniels* tasted like gasoline…it just wasn't done!

Reaching twenty-one had the magical effect of giving me legal status when it came to being around alcohol. Drinking was certainly not a job requirement, although it helped to be able to join in on after-work activities that involved the stuff. I had yet to be invited to join that club. But the most important reason to be legal was; many of the social events covered by the paper served liberal amounts of alcohol. Nashville was still in its infancy when it came to allowing under age persons to be exposed to that particular vice.

Alcohol held little attraction for me. My only experience with it consisted of a few gin and Kool-aide drinks consumed in the basement of a high-school classmate's house, while her parents were away. That particular combination of ingredients, which would likely only appeal to someone who had no business touching alcohol in any form anyway, left me with a sick stomach, spinning head, and the resolve to never consume anything alcoholic ever again. That resolve lasted more than a few years, so the concern about not letting my pre-legal age self in the vicinity of people consuming alcohol was absolutely unnecessary. I didn't care what society people were drinking. I wanted to know what they were up to and I was finally going to get the chance to find out.

My first real writing assignment was to cover a local event held at the *Belle Meade Mansion*. I had been to the Mansion a couple of times during high school, usually as part of a school-sponsored field trip. We were expected to write an essay on what we learned about the history of the place we were herded through. The Mansion was actually one of my least favorite historical places to visit because it seemed to embody a couple of the things I liked least about the South; the extreme separation between those who have and those who have not, and the not-at-all subtle reminder of our roots in racial disparity.

From a strictly architectural point of view, however, the Mansion was pretty impressive. It consisted of a restored antebellum home built in the mid-1800s on what would eventually become known as a plantation. In the old South, plantations were large farms or estates that typically were used to grow crops of one sort or another. In this case, the mansion had been built to replace a log cabin that stood on land originally used to hunt wild game. As the acquired land grew in size from a couple of hundred acres to well over 5,000, the original cabin was torn down and replaced with something more representative of the growing wealth and grandeur of the estate.

Over time, the hunting grounds were transformed into a working farm that included a blacksmith shop, cotton gin, gristmill, and sawmill. It eventually became the site of an impressive horse racing business. In 1853, Virginian John Harding moved his family into the mansion and gave it the name of Belle Meade, in recognition of the beautiful meadow that it overlooked. At that time, the land also provided housing for over a hundred slaves who worked the plantation. The remnants of those shacks, with their dirt floors and meager dimensions, could still be seen scattered along the perimeter of the property.

I suppose it was easy for many visitors to overlook the disparities of life that occurred when the *Belle Meade Mansion* was at its prime, if the constant flow of paying tourists roaming the grounds and buildings was any indication. But I did not count myself among them. To me, the buildings felt like ghostly reminders of past times that filled my heart with dismay and sent a shiver of cold through me that not even the hottest summer day could shake off. It was with the sense of foreboding to tackle my first official writing assignment for *The Nashville News*.

The story I was assigned to cover was a Christmas Ball with a Victorian theme designed to replicate the grand parties held in the mansion at the end of the 19th century. The Victorian era was a part of British history that marked the period of Queen Victoria's reign from 1837 until her death in 1901. The latter half of that era also coincided with what was known as the Gilded Age in the United States, a name adopted by Mark Twain and Charles Dudley Warner to describe what they considered to be a period of serious social problems disguised by a thin gold gilding. That description certainly fit my impression of what was going on at the Belle Meade event.

The scene I witnessed at the Ball represented an ardent attempt to replicate life in high society during the Victorian period, but with a few concessions to the conveniences of life in 1971. It was attended by over 200 of Nashville's elite. It was an interesting mix of those with old money, whose families had established themselves by financially excelling in their trade and passing the money on to future generations, and the *nouveau riche*, who had acquired their own wealth. There is an old saying that "old money can always tell new money". I couldn't say whether or not that was true. They all looked the same to me, especially clothed in the couture of an era long past. But perhaps they were able to detect subtle indicators among themselves that separated them into the two groups. Maybe the old-moneyed gave off a musty scent, like the smell of fine antiques, whereas the newly rich smelled more like freshly polished wood. Whatever the differences, I was sure they were as able to sniff them out in the same way a good hunting dog could nose out the difference between a fox and a squirrel; they both have a bushy tail, but that's where the resemblance ends!

The women in attendance were dressed in the early Victorian style that was both elaborate and restrictive. The upper part of the garments appeared to pinch to mold them into shape, which was likely a fair description of what they were feeling. Undergarments of that era were made of whalebone and flexible steel. From the waist down, they quickly gained girth through an explosion of multiple layers that rose in the back due to a device called a *bustle*. It baffled me why anyone would agree to be clothed in this manner for even a few hours, much less pay for the privilege of spending an entire evening in such discomfort. I wasn't inclined to much experimentation when it came to style. Jeans and a comfortable shirt were my go-to outfit. On this occasion, I gave in and pulled out one of the prom dresses I had worn in high school, hoping I wouldn't stick out in the midst of all of the high fashion parading around me. I set out for the ball, brandishing my reporter's badge and notebook as a shield against any scornful looks that might come my way.

When I first arrived, the volume in the main ballroom was energetic. It quickly reached a loud crescendo as the crowd grew, aided in part by the swishing sound the women made as they attempted to move around to the tunes flowing from the bandstand. Some couples were scouting out seats in the dining area where a buffet feast was being readied. I noticed the women

19

were forced to perch precariously on the edges of their chairs due to the protrusion of the bustles. I had to wonder how they could possibly swallow even a few bites of the delicious looking food, given the squeeze their midsections were likely experiencing. The men seemed to fare much better, which seems to be par for the course, regardless of what time in history one is living. They were mostly decked out in dark gray tailcoats and trousers with white bowties. A few sported the more relaxed combination of pinstriped pants with a dinner jacket. I found it amusing that some of the men went so far as to attach fake mustaches or sideburns to their faces in the style of that long-ago era. Unfortunately, the hairpieces only seemed to come in dark brown, which contrasted sharply with those whose natural color tended towards a lighter or darker shade. The end result was to give them a slightly villainous, but mostly comically theatrical look.

I made my way into a third room designed to resemble a gambling hall. The room was thick with cigar smoke, giving the room the appearance of being fog-covered. Several tables were already filled with men who were simultaneously sucking on stogies and slurping down amber colored liquor. A croupier, who stood at the head of each table, was dealing cards and calling the stakes. The women stood in clusters at the corners of the room looking bored and a little peevish. Tuxedoed waiters passed among them offering champagne and canapés, which the women dived on like famished birds. I suspected many of them were anticipating a long night of standing watch while their dates largely ignored them.

My eyes began to burn from the heavy smoke, so I decided to step outside for a bit of fresh air before making my way back into the main ballroom. I found my way to a patio just outside the back entrance to the Mansion. The air was crisp, which offered a delicious respite from the inside atmosphere, so I pulled out a shawl I had tucked inside my satchel and wrapped it tightly around me. There were a few couples scattered around the patio sipping drinks or enjoying a cigarette. I spotted a concrete bench off to one side and limped my way over to it. The shoes I chose to wear for my inaugural writing assignment, were recommended by the salesman as both stylish and comfortable. I had to admit they were cute, but after an hour of standing on toes cramped into their pointed ends, I was dying to trade them for my well-worn sneakers. I sat on the bench and attempted to massage the cramp out of my right foot when I unexpectedly found myself immersed in shadow.

"I don't envy women having to go through all of that."

I turned to see a tall man standing in the light of a lantern that had previously given a warm glow to my bench seat. I couldn't make out his features in the dim light, but I could see he had dark hair that matched the blackness of his tuxedo and was slicked back with some sort of pomade. Since his outfit was more similar to the servers than the male guests, I assumed he was a waiter who had come to offer me a beverage.

"Do you have any ginger ale?" I asked.

He looked at me with a smirk, then bent at the waist to peer at me quizzically. "No. But you're welcome to share my scotch if you'd like." He held his half-empty glass in my direction.

I frowned at his extended hand. "Are you supposed to be drinking on the job? Aren't you worried about getting caught?"

He straightened sharply producing a sound that could only be called a snort. "You think I'm a waiter." His dark eyes seemed to bore into me as he peered at me more closely, a smirk pulling up the corners of his mouth. I couldn't tell if he was miffed at my assumption of his status or if he just thought I was ridiculous.

I waved my hand toward the other men visible on the porch. "Well, you have to admit you're not dressed like one of the guests. What was I supposed to think?"

He chuckled. "You're supposed to think that an attractive man came over to talk to you. And, by the way, you're not exactly dressed for the part either." He gestured towards my gown with his drinking hand. "What is that, vintage 1965?"

I could feel heat flooding my cheeks, but I wasn't sure if it was from embarrassment over my mistake, or anger at his obvious slam at my dress. All I knew was that I wanted to get away from this man as soon as possible. "Look. I don't know who you are. I'm sorry if I offended you by mistaking you for a waiter, but I have to get back to work now. If you'll excuse me." I stood to leave, attempting to appear as cool as possible, which was no small feat considering I was still holding one shoe in my hand.

He reached out, taking my arm to steady me. "Forgive my rudeness. My name's Jon Barnett, and I'm the one who should be sorry. I'm afraid I have a bad habit of teasing attractive women, especially those who appear to be an easy target for it. If you'll let me help you into that shoe, I promise to leave Cinderella alone for the remainder of the Ball."

I pulled my arm away from him and sat so I could squeeze into my shoe. "That won't be necessary. As I said, I have to get back to work." I could see him glancing inquisitively at the badge that had been hidden by my shawl until I leaned forward to replace my shoe.

"A reporter. Well, that explains it." His demeanor seemed to suddenly cool and his lips were squeezed into a tight line. "I'll leave you to it then." He tipped his drink in my direction before turning to walk nonchalantly back into the mansion.

"What was that about?" I wondered out loud. "Men!" Not that I knew that much about men. I had never been one of the popular girls in high school. I reached my full adult height by the time I was a freshman, but it took three more years for the rest of my body to catch up. As a result, my usual role at social functions had been to take my place in the string of girls lining the gymnasium wall, hoping to catch the eye of some boy who would honor us with a dance. *Wallflowers*, we were called. I suppose the name was intended to soften the blow of unpopularity that we were cast into, but it made me think of weeds waiting to be plucked, then discarded when something prettier showed up. I hated attending such events, but had to succumb to being dropped off by my parents who nodded at me resignedly each time. They didn't bother to hide their disappointment when they returned to find me waiting alone at the end of the evening. Mind you, I did have a few dates in high school, but they tended to be with boys who were also misfits in one way or another; the geeks, the closet gays, the boys who would likely be adorable in several years, but currently sported a patina of adolescent pimples that marred their potential looks.

Since high school, there had been only the occasional blind date with someone's cousin from out of town or brother who needed a *plus one* to some party. I wasn't what you would call experienced at relating to the opposite sex. Jon Barnett was one of those men who looked like he never had to work hard to find a date in his life, the type that always brought out my insecurity. His sudden exit suggested he had figured out I wasn't worth his time. *Not that I cared*, I told myself, knowing deep inside it wasn't true.

I stood and attempted to smooth out the wrinkles that had settled into my skirt. I decided to head to the ladies' room to see if I could eavesdrop on some juicy gossip that just might lead me to a story line. At least, that was one of the few pluses about being a social wallflower; people tended not to notice you were around.

Chapter 3

The next day, I practically jumped out of bed before my alarm went off. I rented a one bedroom, one bath, furnished apartment shortly after securing my job on *The Nashville News*. It wasn't very fancy, but it was located in an interesting part of town known as Music Row, due to the large number of recording studios and other music businesses in the area. It was also only a short drive from my work, which was a huge plus when it came to budgeting for the cost of gasoline and the other myriad expenses that seemed to be constantly necessary to keep my old VW bug running.

My apartment was small; tiny by some standards, but it had floor-to-ceiling windows on one side that flanked a small balcony which allowed the room to fill with natural light on even the cloudiest of days. The balcony was one of my favorite places. The street noise made a pleasant backdrop for reading or thinking, and I could frequently catch strains of music drifting from one of the nearby studios. Music people were a colorful bunch. It was fun to watch the changing parade of characters moving in and out of the buildings as they beat a path from one hope-filled spot to the next. Hope, of course, was the daily diet of music business *wannabees*; the constantly changing group of musicians, songwriters, and composers who piled into Nashville in hopes of being "discovered" and welcomed into the ranks of the rich and famous. There were a lot of dashed dreams walking around the streets of Nashville.

The building that housed my apartment was four stories high. My unit was located at the rear of the top floor. There was no elevator, which was fairly common for buildings in the area, but which also provided a real challenge during my weekly haul of groceries or laundry. Each level of the building contained a hallway to six apartments. The newspaper delivery guy had the habit of tossing the daily paper up through the staircase from the bottom level. I could only guess this was done in order to shorten his delivery time. But my paper often landed in front of someone else's door, if it managed to end up on my level at all. Luckily, today it was balanced neatly against my front door.

I snatched the paper and carried it into the kitchen, eager to see my first-ever official byline from my coverage of the previous night's Ball. I flipped the switch on my coffeepot and tried to ignore the insistent mews emanating from my cat, Ebie…a shortened version of Ebony, which just seemed too formal for such a sweet little girl. She was an adorable, black kitten I brought home from the local animal shelter. She became the love of my life, although I was careful not to announce that to many people. Most mornings, I let her hop up onto my kitchen table to keep me company while I ate my breakfast. A habit I was sure would scare off any potential suitors, not that there had been any in my apartment so far. This morning, she was wrapping herself around my legs as I flipped through the pages. I reached down, scooped her into my lap, and scratched the top of her head.

"I know you're hungry, but you'll have to wait a few more minutes." She settled comfortably across my legs and began to purr. "Ah, here it is." The story was tucked away on page 5 of the local section. I hoped it might earn a more prominent location, but I knew any spot was better than none. "Belle Meade Mansion Hosts Victorian Christmas, by Georgia Ayres," I read aloud. Ebie looked up at me expectantly. "That's right. Your momma is a star." She blinked her eyes at me as if to say, "You are so wonderful! Now, where is my breakfast?" Cats are very expressive that way.

It only took me a few minutes to read through the five paragraphs of my story. I had been limited to a set number of words, and found it difficult to fit more than a rudimentary listing of who, what, when, where, and how…the journalists' creed of content…to the allotted space. Most of the page was filled with photographs of the attendees, which is what everyone looked for anyway. People loved to see themselves in the newspaper. They certainly cared more about how they looked than anything else a fledgling reporter might have to say. Unless, of course, it was to praise how they looked.

I allowed myself a self-pitying sigh before folding the paper and setting Ebie on the floor. "Okay then, that's enough of that." I opened one of the kitchen cabinets and scanned the stack of cat food cans displayed there. "What do you feel like today, Ebie? Tuna? Or would you rather have turkey and cheese?" She responded with what I thought of as her happy dance, which involved alternately weaving herself between my legs and standing on her hind feet as she attempted to reach the countertop. "Tuna it is then." It's true that tuna was her favorite, but I had to admit I tended to choose the flavor that most appealed to me at the time. I opened the can and spooned it into her bowl, then poured a cup of coffee for myself.

Two hours later, I was back in the familiar surroundings of the newsroom, after having first delivered the daily orders of coffee, soft drinks, and donuts to everyone from the proofreaders to the editor-in-chief. It seemed my initiation into becoming a real reporter had not changed my role as a gopher. I was still expected to go for whatever refreshments the rest of the staff requested. I was beginning to learn the hard truth that working for a newspaper was like working in any other political arena; it was all about the tug of war over who gets what, when, and how. Some politics involved the struggle for power between groups. The newspaper world revolved around the struggle of individuals vying for status and recognition. I had never been much of a political animal, preferring instead to keep my head down and avoid conflict. But I could see that was going to have to change if I intended to hold my own in the newspaper profession.

As I made my way through the maze of the newsroom to my desk in the far back left corner, I thought about how the layout was like a small city. Instead of using buildings and highways to create a viable matrix, this office city was mapped out with desks and workspaces linked together to create a sort of communication grid. At first glance, this arrangement appeared to be chaotic, but it allowed a quick exchange of information between the various staff members as they responded to story leads tossed their way from the assignment editors.

The assignment editors were the traffic controllers of the newsroom. Their job was to monitor scanners, fax machines, and phone lines that were constantly coughing out facts, then decide what was newsworthy and assign a reporter to cover the story. Their desk was raised a few steps above the rest of the newsroom to make it easy to shout out assignments. There was a sort of unofficial ranking created by how near one's desk was to the assignment desk, since those reporters who were closest usually received the choicest stories. Unfortunately, my desk was about as far away as you could get, without actually being outside the building.

The communal layout of the room also created a rather loud cacophony of sounds, ranging from the rat-a-tat of typewriter keys, to the shouted questions tossed from one workstation to another. There was also a unique odor to the mix that came from the cloud of cigarette and cigar smoke that wafted across the room like fog on a misty day. It mixed with undertones of cologne and shaving cream, and something that I guessed came from the silver flasks not-too-discretely tucked inside the top desk drawers of many of the more seasoned reporters. It wasn't an altogether unpleasant atmosphere to work in, but it took a few hours each evening for my ears to stop ringing, and I had to hang my clothes on the balcony overnight before I could stand to be in the same room with them.

The rest of the day was uneventful, which was a bit of a let-down in the aftermath of my moment of glory, as I thought of it. I had yet to be given another assignment, but I told myself it was because there wasn't much going on in the Nashville local scene. That's the way the news went; sometimes it poured in like hot, molten chocolate oozing with deliciousness; other times it was as cold as ice on a metal pole in the dead of winter. Just as I was about to pack it in for the day, the city editor and my boss, Don Williams, yelled across the room to me.

"Ayres. Chief wants to see you." He jerked his head in the direction of the editor-in-chief's office. In alarm, I almost dropped the stack of papers I was holding. The editor-in-chief was a stodgy, balding, cigar-chewing man in his late fifties who reminded me of Lou Grant on the *Mary Tyler Moore Show*. But whereas the sitcom character had a certain teddy bear like lovability about him, Ralph Stein reminded me more of a grizzly bear that had just been awakened from its winter hibernation.

His office was located at the front of the room, and I could feel my heart pounding as I made my way in that direction. His door was shut when I arrived. Even the blinds covering the glass walls surrounding the room were pulled tight. I knocked quietly and heard a gruff voice reply, "Come in." He was sitting at his desk with his head bent over a stack of copy and he waved me to a chair without looking up. After an uncomfortable few seconds, he glanced up at me.

"You want to explain this?" He nodded towards the corner of his desk where a bottle-shaped package sat. It was wrapped in silver paper with a red bow tied around the neck.

"I—don't know what you mean." I looked back and forth from him to the package in confusion.

"Does the name Jon Barnett ring a bell?" He removed his glasses and tossed them on the desk before leaning back in his chair.

I sat up a little straighter in my chair. "I met him last night at the Ball. I mean, he started talking to me out of the blue, then he just walked off." I looked at the package with more interest. "Is that from him?"

He thrust the package in my direction. "See for yourself. There's a card. I already read it because it's my job to keep an eye on everything that goes on around here."

I opened the card and read the words out loud. "Sorry for my abrupt departure last night. Hope this can make up for my rudeness. Jon Barnett." I tore the paper off to reveal a bottle of ginger ale. I couldn't help but smile at the memory of my mistake from the previous evening, and found myself feeling a little less peeved at how our encounter ended.

"You want to explain that?" He asked me again.

"I thought he was a waiter so I asked him for a ginger ale. He left rather suddenly when he saw my reporter's badge. I guess this is his way of apologizing."

Ralph's necktie seemed to be cutting off the circulation to his neck because his face had begun to turn a deep shade of red. "Do you have any idea who he is?" I shook my head "no". "His family owns the largest newspaper publishing company in the United States. They've been buying up a lot of local and national papers, taking over their management. Some people say their intent is to kill the industry. Others think it could be the best thing that ever happened to the newspaper business. Their company headquarters is based in D.C., which means that Barnett's a long way from home. It can't be pure coincidence that he shows up in Nashville at the same time our two local papers are struggling for survival. His reaction to finding out you're a reporter suggests he might not want to broadcast his reason for being here. All I know for sure is this guy is not someone you want to mess around with."

The two papers he was referring to were *The Daily Courier* and *The Nashville News*. They were longtime rivals in the Nashville community. While the *Courier* tended to take a conservative, Republican stance on most issues, *The Nashville News* leaned towards a more liberal, Democratic point of view. At the present time, the two papers were sharing space in the same building on Broadway in downtown Nashville. Their tumultuous relationship made for a very strained atmosphere in the building. The only thing that saved the respective staff members from breaking out into a flat-out fist fight was *The Nashville News* was printed for delivery in the morning, while *The Daily Courier* was readied for the afternoon. As a result, there was less physical overlap among the two staffs than there could have been.

I considered what he was suggesting. "I assure you I wasn't 'messing around with him', as you put it. As I said, he approached me. We talked a little. Then he left. That's all there was to it." As the words left my mouth, I gulped down my surprise at my boldness in speaking up for myself.

His eyes narrowed as he began to chew on the end of his reading glasses.

"Maybe we can turn this around to our advantage. This silly little gift does seem to be his way of trying to apologize for taking off on you. Maybe you should use it as an excuse to get in touch with him."

I looked at him with alarm. "But I thought you said I should steer clear of him. I wouldn't have the slightest idea how to contact him."

"You're a reporter, right? Figure it out." He stood abruptly and opened the door to his office, which was my cue to leave.

I walked quickly back to my desk and collected my things. Once I was outside the building, I took a deep breath. "Whew! That was crazy!" My head was spinning from our exchange. I never found it pleasant to be on the receiving end of an inquisition, which was exactly what I felt like I had just been through. Now I was faced with the daunting task of not only finding the enigmatic Mr. Barnett, but of soothing any of his feathers I may have ruffled during our last meeting. I walked to my car and tossed my pocketbook and satchel in the back seat. My plan was to head straight home and change into walking clothes so I could try to shake off some of my accumulated tension. My best friend, Julie, might be home by then, too. She was my sounding board whenever I needed to work something through my brain. This situation with Jon Barnett was definitely something I could use help sorting out.

Chapter 4

I stepped out on my balcony the next morning to find that a snow sky had moved in overnight. A *snow sky* is what I called it when the sky becomes covered in so much puffy whiteness that it looks like the clouds are certain to open a shower of snow. I wasn't always right in my prediction, but this time the air also carried that telltale scent of cold dampness that quite often preceded the arrival of snow. Besides, the local weather report had called for it, too. Although they weren't known for their accuracy, it was January in Nashville, and we were overdue for a good blanket of winter wonder.

A snowy Sunday suited me just fine. It was rare for me to have a whole day that I didn't have to go into work. I relished the idea of easing into this one with a warm mug of coffee, some tunes playing on my radio, and, of course, the Sunday paper. I pulled the comforter from my bed and hauled it to the living room sofa where I could keep watch on the weather through the sliding glass doors of my balcony. Ebie quickly joined me and settled her tiny body snugly against my legs.

After an hour of luxuriating in my laziness, I was trying to decide between taking a nap and pouring one more cup of coffee, when the phone rang. "Oh, drat!" Ebie leapt from her spot next to my leg looking at me as if to ask, "Why did you wake me?" I only had one phone in my apartment. It was on the wall in the kitchen, which meant I had to follow Ebie's example and pull myself up from the cozy warmth of my comforter to get to it.

"Hello?"

"Oh! I'm sorry. Did I wake you?" It was my good friend Julie.

"Almost. I was just thinking about going back to sleep." I settled into one of the chairs at the kitchen table. "What are you up to?" The temperature in the kitchen was chilly, and I shifted in my chair to try to tuck my feet under me. Flexibility had never been my strong suit, and I finally gave up and propped my feet on the tabletop.

"Remember what we were talking about last night? About how your boss told you to track down that guy from the party?" I had stopped by Julie's after my post-work walk and we ended up talking for hours. That's the way it always was with us; we talked to each other almost every day, but we never seemed to run out of things to talk about. "Well, have you looked at the morning paper?"

I chuckled. "You're asking an employee of the newspaper if she's read the morning paper? Actually, I've only made it through the first section and the comics so far."

"Well, go get the Local News section and turn to page 3." I put down the phone and retrieved the section she was referring to. As I passed in front of the sofa, I noticed big, fat flakes of snow had begun to fall outside, and stick to the balcony floor. I sat at the kitchen table and opened to the page she mentioned. A photo in the top right corner caught my eye. There was the man I had met at the Ball shaking the hand of an older man sporting a pencil-thin mustache. I recognized the older man as the mayor of Nashville, Bradford Brill. He was smiling, but Jon Barnett appeared grim by comparison. The caption over the photo read "Mayor Appoints New Member to Metropolitan Historical Commission". The article attached to the photo went on to say that Mayor Brill was appointing Jon Barnett to the voluntary commission. It was created in Nashville in 1966 to document the history of the city, save and reuse buildings, and increase the public's awareness of the advantages of preserving history.

"That's interesting. I guess he's planning on staying in town for a while." I was surprised to find the idea of Jon Barnett staying in Nashville didn't entirely upset me, despite Mr. Stein's warnings about him. His dark eyes had a way of capturing my attention, even when they were just looking at me from a black and white photo.

I guess I was staring at his image a little too long because I heard Julie's voice. "Earth to Georgia! Are you still there, or has the image of Mr. Gorgeous made you speechless?" Julie had a way of always reading me like a book; a trait I found both irritating and endearing. On this occasion, I decided to ignore her insinuation.

"I'm just thinking about what Mr. Stein said; about how it's my job now to find him and smooth things over. I guess this article means I won't have to look too far." I suddenly found myself anxious to get off the phone. I needed some time to think things through, to figure out what I would say if I saw Jon Barnett again, and to understand why the prospect of seeing him made my heart beat a little faster. "Listen, Julie, I've got to go. There are some things I need to take care of before work tomorrow."

"Hum. I've never known you to want to think about work on your day off. You sure you're not just trying to change the subject?"

"Maybe a little, but I really do need to go. I'll call you later."

After I hung up, I took another look at the photo of Jon Barnett. He certainly was handsome, in a polished, movie star sort of way. Exactly the type of handsome that never gave me a second look. Besides, the man was very likely going to put me out of a job, if Mr. Stein's hunch about him was correct. That sounded like a combination that could only result in trouble. *Trouble* was something I made every effort to avoid.

I sighed and tossed the paper on the kitchen table. I needed to focus my attention on one thing. I had an assignment from the Chief, and if I wanted to keep my job, I damn well better figure out how to do it right. I took one more longing look at my comforter, which had now been commandeered by Ebie who was stretched as far as possible into its warm folds. I reached into my work satchel for a pen and notepad. Maybe I could sketch out some ideas for an article I could write on the Historical Commission. That might be just the angle I could use to approach Jon Barnett. It would also keep our next meeting completely professional. At least, that's what I told myself.

Chapter 5

I awoke the next morning to a bona fide snow day. At least four inches had fallen overnight, making everything look coated in vanilla icing. The sun shone brightly, giving the impression of warmth. I stuck my head out my balcony door and felt the icy chill, quickly realizing most of Nashville would likely stay socked in at home all day. The city wasn't very well prepared to deal with winter weather, since it happened so rarely. As a result, schools tended to announce their closure at the first hint of ice or snow; grocery store shelves were ravaged of every imaginable food necessity. Work places were prone to discourage employees from coming in, unless it was absolutely necessary. Not so with the newspaper business. We were in the same boat as the mailmen who promised to bring us our bills and letters regardless of rain or snow or sleet or hail or gloom of night. In our case, we had to get out the paper so all those housebound citizens would still know what had been going on in the world while they were sleeping.

I looked down at the street to see my VW bug barely recognizable under its snow cover. It would be quite a job to dig it out, and there was a good chance it wouldn't start. *Tweedledee,* a name I chose from one of my favorite characters in *Alice in Wonderland*, with whom the car shared a lot of physical similarities...was sensitive to both cold and heat. I never knew from one day to the next if he would start at all. On more than one occasion, I had been forced to walk the six blocks to the newspaper building after futile attempts to get it started. I was becoming fast friends with the local AAA staff who had rescued me more than once. I knew sooner or later I would need to dig into my meager savings for a new battery, but I had been putting it off in hopes I might actually be able to trade *Tweedledee* for a newer old car instead.

Given the weather conditions outside, I decided the most sensible thing for me to do would be to just walk to work. I dug through my closet for a pair of rain boots I thought would work better than my sneakers and set them next to the front door. I took a quick wash and began pulling on layers of clothing in an attempt to brace myself for dealing with the icy cold outside.

A pair of long underwear went on first, followed by knee length wool socks, corduroy pants, a cotton turtleneck, and a wool sweater. I completed my ensemble with a wool scarf, stocking cap, gloves, and a parka. The finished result made me think of what the *Pillsbury Doughboy* would look like dressed as an Eskimo.

I waddled my way over to the door and pushed my right foot into a rubber boot only to hear a loud "Yeeooowww!" I yanked my foot from the boot followed quickly by Ebie who scrambled out and stared back at me with a look of wide-eyed shock.

"I'm sorry! I didn't know you were in there." I attempted to pick her up to soothe her but she scampered out of reach under the sofa. I bent down so I could see her face. "I said I'm sorry. But you weren't supposed to be in my boot." We had only been roommates for about three months, so I guess we weren't at the stage yet where she knew she could trust me unconditionally. I gave one final, futile attempt to reach her and decided any reconciliation would have to wait until I returned. I checked her food and water dishes to make sure they were full and added a couple of kitty treats to the top of her dry food. They were intended as a sort of apology, to make *me* feel better.

As I predicted, the roads were a mess of slushy snow and ice. There were very few people out and about, and I was sort of enjoying having the city to myself. But my pleasure was dampened by the struggle I was having pushing my way through snow that threatened to seep down into the top of my boots. There was actually more snow on the sidewalks than the roads because the plow trucks had been steadfastly pushing most of the snow from the streets onto the sides of the road.

My rubber boots made a sucking sound as I trudged along. I was heating up quickly from the effort, forcing me to loosen my scarf and unbutton my parka. I was beginning to wish I hadn't piled on so many layers of clothing as I felt the sweat trickle down my back. After about 30 minutes, I finally made my way to the entrance of the newspaper offices on Broadway. I pushed my way through the front door, and noticed that despite the outside conditions, everything seemed to be business as usual inside. I was greeted by the familiar sound of typewriters amidst the discord of several people talking at once.

I squished my way to my desk and plopped down in the chair so I could pull my boots off. I had tucked a pair of regular shoes in my satchel and I slipped my feet into them, luxuriating in the feel of warm comfort. I yanked off my cap, scarf, parka, and wool sweater and tossed them over a file cabinet next to my desk. I was considering retreating to the restroom to remove my long underwear when the city editor showed up.

"'Bout time you got here. Got a story for you." He handed me a folded page from the Sunday edition of *The Nashville News*. I opened the page excitedly, wondering what assignment I had been given. My face fell as I saw the picture of the Mayor and Jon Barnett. Apparently, the only news assignments I could expect in the near future were going to come from my fateful encounter with Mr. Barnett. It was clear I was going to have to deal with this quickly, if I wanted to be thought of as worthy of reporting on anything else.

"Actually, I have a few ideas about this." I pulled my notepad from my satchel and flipped open the cover. "I'd like to look into the background of this Commission he's been appointed to. See what it has to do with him and, more importantly, what it has to do with his family's involvement in newspaper publishing. I have a hunch they are somehow connected."

Don nodded his head at me. "Then you'd best be putting all that paraphernalia back on again." He gestured toward my pile of winter clothes. "The office of the Historical Commission is in the Stahlman Building down on the corner of Third and Union. Everything you want to know about the MHC can be found there."

"But do you think there'd be anyone there today? Given the weather, I mean."

He turned and started to walk away. "Only one way to find out. Give 'em a call."

Right, I thought. Newspaper people, especially editors, weren't known for being great conversationalists. You'd think anyone who dealt all day with words would have an affinity for verbal expression, but that wasn't usually the case. Maybe their craft required them to use as few words as possible to get across their point. Whatever the reason, it was clear I was going to have to figure out most things on my own.

Chapter 6

My efforts at reaching anyone at the MHC were futile, which did not surprise me. Most of the news that day was about the snowstorm, and its effect on everyone and everything that attempted to maneuver about the city. Things finally began to clear up considerably three days later so I decided to walk down to the Stahlman building to see if I could find anyone in the MHC office.

The building was an impressive gray stone structure that rose twelve stories tall, and featured a line of Roman columns across its front. An article I had uncovered in the news archives indicated it had been built in 1907, at which time it ranked as only one of two skyscrapers in the city. The other was the equally tall J.C. Bradford building at the corner of Fourth and Church Streets.

Originally, the Stahlman building was known as a banking establishment, although the banking area only occupied the bottom floor. Over the years, it also became home to numerous law offices and civil courts, likely due to its close proximity to the courthouse. That was all before my time. My memories of the Stahlman had to do with a local radio station that made sure its presence was known by the 8 feet tall backlit call letters on the top of the building. This made the rooftop of the Stahlman a beacon to guide both low-flying aircraft as well as locals attempting to orient themselves through the maze of downtown streets. I had actually been to the top of the Stahlman a couple of times when I was in high school because it had the reputation of affording the best view of the city. I have to admit the view was impressive.

In recent years, the Metro government purchased the building and made it home to various government agencies and commissions, including the historical commission. As I entered the main lobby, I noticed a placard describing how the building had been named after the newspaper publisher, Edward Stahlman, who started *The Daily Courier* in 1890, and whose family still owned the existing *Courier*. *The Daily Courier* lacked any strong competition in the Nashville area until *The Nashville News* was launched in 1907. That was the same year the Stahlman was built, causing me to wonder if the location of the Commission, and Jon Barnett's appointment to it, was more than a coincidence.

I scanned a list of offices posted next to the elevators, spotting The Metropolitan Historical Commission on the fourth floor. When I reached that floor, the elevator doors opened onto a long hallway with closed doors on either side. I could hear the faint sound of music from somewhere so I followed the sound to a door labeled Metropolitan Historical Commission and knocked quietly. I wasn't sure if my unannounced visit would be welcome, and I was halfway hoping no one would answer my knock. Just as I was about to turn away, the door opened slightly to reveal a short, gray-haired woman, who peered out at me curiously. Her hair was pulled into two buns on either side of her head that framed a pair of dark, horn-rimmed glasses. The glasses made her eyes appear enormous, and I found it difficult to pull myself away from them; she continued to stare at me with a curious but friendly smile.

"Yes? Did you want something, dear?" She wore a gray skirt and sweater set, and a neatly ironed white blouse with a scalloped collar. Her feet were covered in sturdy black leather shoes that were polished to a high gloss. A name badge clipped to her sweater read *Ida Hood*. She reminded me more than a little of my own grandmother, Nanna, and I found myself fighting back emotions as I looked at her. Nanna had been my staunch supporter during my rather tumultuous childhood years, particularly during the last few years of her life when she lived in a small room on the main floor of our house. Whenever I would find myself on the wrong side with either of my parents, I would make a fast escape to her room, never failing to find solace in the comfort of her warm hugs and stash of cookies. We never spoke about the circumstances that caused me to regularly seek refuge in her company, but I knew she was aware of how difficult life with my parents could be. It was only after she was gone that I wished I had spoken to her more freely about my feelings.

I felt myself stand straighter, as if it was actually Nanna I was addressing. "Excuse my poor manners. My name is Georgia Ayres. I'm a reporter with *The Nashville News*. I was interested in talking to someone about a recent volunteer who the mayor appointed to the Commission."

Her smile seemed to fade. "Oh yes. You must mean Mr. Barnett. What was it you wanted to know about him?"

"You know him? Do you know where I can find him?"

She sighed quietly and turned to walk into the room. I wasn't sure whether or not to follow her, so I remained standing in the doorway. Finally, she looked back over her shoulder. "You should probably come in. It will take me a few minutes to find what you need."

I closed the door quietly behind me. It was a fairly small space, made even smaller by the clutter of filing cabinets, desks, and chairs crammed closely together. There were two large windows along one wall which allowed a welcome amount of sunlight into the otherwise dim space. I noticed someone had positioned two chairs and a small table in front of the windows in order to take advantage of the light.

Miss Hood gestured to one of the chairs. "Why don't you have a seat? I just made some coffee if you'd like some." She pointed to where a coffee pot rested on top of one of the cabinets surrounded by an array of mismatched cups, and a radio from which emanated the music that had drawn me down the hall. The coffee smelled good. I decided not to take her up on her offer, since I wasn't sure how long I would be staying.

The room was warm, and I started to loosen my coat and scarf as I sat. I scanned the room for any hints about the work of the Commission. A small stack of pamphlets lay on the desk nearest to where I sat, and I grabbed the top one. It had a picture of the Belmont Mansion located on the campus of Belmont College, which was just a short distance from my apartment. I had driven past it many times. I was always curious about its history, but had never taken the time to learn anything about it.

The pamphlet described how Joseph and Adelicia Acklen built the Mansion in 1853. It was designed to resemble an Italian villa, with its lush setting and pastoral views; and was referred to as Belle Monte by the Acklens.

The pamphlet told how the mansion was sold to two female teachers from Philadelphia in 1890 following the death of both Adelicia and her third husband, Dr. William Cheatham. The women established Belmont College for Young Women on 15-acres of the original property. In 1913, the college was merged with Ward Seminary for Young Ladies, which had been opened in Nashville in 1865. The combined schools became Ward-Belmont, the first junior college in the South to receive full accreditation by the Southern Association of Colleges and Secondary Schools. The junior college was sold in 1951 to the Tennessee Baptist Convention, which restored the title of Belmont College to what was then a co-educational institution of learning.

The final paragraph of the pamphlet contained a photo of the two women, Susan L. Heron and Ida E. Hood, responsible for starting Belmont College. My eyes opened wide when I saw the names. "This is about you!" I held the pamphlet up for her to see. "You're Ida Hood!"

She turned to see what I was holding and laughed out loud. "I know I'm old, but really now, do you think it would be possible for me to still be standing if I was over 100?" She took the pamphlet from me and smiled at the picture on the cover. "The

43

original Belmont College was started by my father's spinster sister and her friend. I was named for her. I guess I followed in her footsteps, because I never married either. When I learned what she had done to help young women have a place to develop their minds, I was proud to carry her name. She chuckled to herself. "It's even possible it may have influenced my decision not to take someone else's name a time or two, although I guess I could have been persuaded if I had really set my cap for the fellow. Truth is, my head had always been so filled with stories about my aunt's adventures I was dead set on having some of my own. I even attended Belmont College for a while when I was in my twenties. That was when it was a junior college by the name of Ward-Belmont. But I had wanderlust in my blood, and I left school after my second year to see the world." She handed the pamphlet back to me and shook her head with a wistful look. "Turned out that everything I was looking for was right here."

I was tempted to ask her what she meant, but something made me hold back. "So now you work for the Historical Commission." I said it as a statement, but I was really hoping she'd recognize the question I really wanted to ask. Unfortunately, she suddenly seemed anxious for me to go.

"This may help you with what you came for." She handed me a piece of paper with a list of names and phone numbers of the MHC volunteers. A quick scan of the list revealed that Jon Barnett was among them.

"Yes. Thank you very much. This should be helpful." I started to pull on my coat but I felt a hand on my arm.

"Be careful, Miss Ayres. Don't ask questions if you are not prepared to hear the answers."

I was puzzled by her comment and again wished I felt free enough to ask for an explanation. But there was something in her eyes that said I should let it alone. She removed her hand from my arm as quickly as she had placed it there.

"Mind your footing when you get back outside. You know what they say about black ice; you can't see it until you're flat on your face on top of it." She smiled warmly and held the door open for me to leave.

"Thank you, for everything." The unspoken hung between us with a heaviness that was palpable. I couldn't wait to leave the room, yet at the same time, something pulled at me to stay. Since the open door left me only one choice, I nodded my goodbye.

Chapter 7

It was several days before I was able to follow up on the lead Miss Hood had given me. Life has a way of getting filled up with all sorts of things, although I suspect most of what I allowed to pass for being busy was really just wasted time. I was intentionally dragging my feet on getting in contact with Jon Barnett. There was just something about Miss Hood's demeanor when I mentioned his name, not to mention the warning that she gave me as I left her office, which left me with a feeling of uneasiness. I had been getting pointed looks from my boss for some time, and I knew I couldn't put off the encounter any longer. I placed a call to the contact number listed on the sheet Miss Hood had given me. To my surprise, the phone was answered after two rings.

"Barnett here."

I wasn't expecting him to actually answer the phone, and I was momentarily struck speechless.

"Hello? Is anyone there?" He sounded somewhat annoyed, which, based on our previous encounter, I imagined may have been pretty much in character for him.

"Oh, hello Mr. Barnett. My name is Georgia Ayres. I'm a reporter for *The Nashville News*. We actually met at an event at the Belle Meade Mansion."

"I know who you are Miss Ayres." The tone of his voice had shifted from gruff to flirty. "Did you enjoy my gift?"

I smiled at the memory. "It was certainly unique. Although it got me in a bit of hot water with my Editor-in-chief."

"You mean he didn't approve of the gift or the gift-giver?" He chuckled, but I could tell he was a bit put off by the insinuation.

I realized I should have been more prepared before I placed the call. I could feel the heat of embarrassment flooding my face. I needed to find a way to smooth things over quickly before they escalated into a situation that would get me in even more trouble with Mr. Stein. After all, he had instructed me to be friendly with Mr. Barnett as a means of finding out what he was up to. Unfortunately, my inexperience in dealing with the opposite sex, in particular one who was as attractive and apparently worldly as Jon Barnett, left me struggling to find an appropriate reply. Luckily, he must have sensed my discomfort because his voice became friendly again.

"I'm sorry. That was rude of me. Again. I seem to find myself apologizing to you too often. You obviously called because you wanted something. What can I help you with?"

"Oh. I just wanted to thank you for the gift. I mean it was nice of you to remember me, especially since I mistook you for a waiter. I'm surprised you didn't send me a bar of soap so I could wash my mouth out."

He laughed heartily. "Perhaps that would have been more appropriate, but I was the one who walked away.

His apology was unexpected. This man had a way of raising my hackles in one moment, then turning me to warm jelly in the next. I couldn't decide what to make of him or his mixed messages. I decided to turn the conversation around to see if I could find out why he was in Nashville, and what his appointment to the Commission had to do with his family's intent to acquire newspapers, perhaps even our own *Nashville News*. I decided an indirect approach would probably be smarter than trying to broach these issues head-on, prone as I was to putting my size 9 foot in my mouth.

"As I said, I really just called to thank you, and I wondered if you would be interested in meeting me for a cup of coffee sometime? We both sort of got off on the wrong foot with each other. I thought it might be nice to start over."

There was a pause on the line as if he was considering how to respond. Just as I was beginning to question the wisdom of my suggestion, he spoke up. "I never turn down an invitation to meet a pretty lady. But let's make it lunch. How about tomorrow? I have a meeting downtown that I should be out of by noon. Why don't we meet at this chili spot I've heard about; *Varallo's*. Do you know it?"

I was a little taken aback by his quick acceptance of my invitation. I again wished I had thought through my plan more carefully before rushing in unprepared. "Sure. Everybody knows *Varallo's*. It's a Nashville tradition, and a hot spot for locals and the occasional unsuspecting out-of-towner. But I have to warn you. There could be quite a wait to get in there at that time of the day. I've seen a line two blocks long sometimes. Their 3-way chili is famous." Their reputation for being a hotbed of controversy was even more so, but I didn't mention that. *Varallo's* was known as a favorite spot for under the table deals and off-the-record agreements between some of Nashville's best-known businessmen, including an array of political powerhouses. On any given week, anyone who was anyone on the political scene was sure to be spotted in *Varallo's*. Whenever there was an election campaign in progress, a bevy of reporters made their rounds of the lunch crowd hoping to pick up on which way the vote was likely to go. It was odd that Jon Barnett would pick that particular spot for lunch, and it further piqued my curiosity about exactly what he was up to. I decided the best way to find out was to feign ignorance.

"Our editor-in-chief is an old friend of the owner. Let me see if he can make a call to get us a table. They don't advertise the fact, but it's pretty well known that some people get special treatment when it comes to bypassing the line waiting to get in."

"It's a date then, but only if you agree to call me Jon. Mr. Barnett makes me sound so old."

I wasn't sure I was comfortable with him calling our lunch meeting a date, but I decided not to press the issue. After all, I wanted to keep my real purpose in meeting him a secret. That's what a good reporter would do. But in truth, I was beginning to doubt just how good a reporter I was, especially when it came to staying focused on my real reason for seeing Jon Barnett again.

Chapter 8

I arrived at *Varallo's* promptly at noon and was surprised to see Jon perched on a stool at the counter in deep conversation with the owner's wife, Evelyn. Evelyn's role in the restaurant was to serve as the hostess, cashier, and all-around ambassador of goodwill. It was a role she performed to perfection. Her quick wit and warm nature were a natural complement to her husband, Francesco's, stoic charm. On this day, Francesco was manning the steam table, decked out in his customary toque and bowtie, dishing out the day's offerings of meat and vegetables. It was a well-loved tradition in Southern restaurants to serve what had become known as a *meat-n- three*, meaning that you could choose a meat from the days' available choices, which often included fried chicken, pork chops, meatloaf, and catfish, then select three of the day's vegetables to go with it. Although *Varallo's* was known for its chili, the owners were wise enough to realize a daily bowl of the mixture, regardless of how delicious it tasted, wouldn't be to everyone's liking. As they had correctly guessed, the addition of the steam table offerings had doubled the size of their daily crowds.

Jon spotted me as I entered the dining room and waved me over. "Georgia. My meeting ended earlier than I expected, so Mrs. Varallo has been keeping me company while I waited for you. Did you know she's a famous singer?"

Evelyn's eyes twinkled behind her horn-rimmed glasses as she looked over at Jon. "Now Mr. Barnett. You know you're making that up. I only said I used to sing in the church choir when I was younger. I don't think my voice would have made anyone sit up and take notice." It was clear she was enjoying Jon's flirtatious banter. Apparently, he had a way with women of all ages, which was not a trait I found especially endearing. Mrs. Varallo smiled at her husband who was standing at the opposite end of the counter. "Except for Francesco, that is. He always says it was my voice that first caught his attention. Of course, he never says if it sounded good or bad."

"You always sound like an angel to me, sweetheart." Francesco tipped his toque at his wife as he placed a hefty ladle of green beans onto a plate.

Evelyn came from behind the counter and stood next to me. "You must be the new young reporter Mr. Stein told me about. I have a table for you two right over here." She led the way through the crowded room to a small table in the corner. Along the way, I noticed a group that included several reporters I recognized from *The Daily Courier*. I nodded in their direction, receiving in return only blank stares and a couple of scowling looks. I wasn't sure if their reaction was due to my being a member of their competition or my gender. Even though a sign in the window proclaimed "Ladies are welcome", most of the tables were filled with male customers.

Jon opened his menu and scanned the available choices. "So, what is this *3-way chili* I've heard so much about?"

I opened my own menu and pointed to the description printed there. "It's chili beans, spaghetti, and a tamale in the same bowl. It's really good."

"Then that's what I'll have." He closed his menu and leaned back in his chair, letting his eyes scan the crowd. "Pretty popular place. I'm glad you suggested it."

His comment surprised me. "Actually, it was your idea. I just suggested we'd need some help to get a table without waiting a long time." We both turned to look at the line that had formed outside the door to the restaurant. The crowds had gotten so bad in the past year the owners had been forced to adopt the policy that no one outside could come in until someone from inside left. They went so far as to lock the door to prevent those who were unfamiliar with the policy from barging their way in. A doorman had been hired to stand at the door to handle the exit and entry of patrons. *Doorman* was a polite way of saying he was a bouncer. Word had it he was a former heavyweight wrestler who the Varallos befriended after he became a regular, late-night diner. Whether this was true or not, his large, imposing frame was quite effective at discouraging impatient diners from making a scene.

The waitress came to take our orders. "3-way chili with a coke for Jon, catfish with greens, creamed corn, and mashed potatoes with sweet tea for me." Jon looked at me expectantly. "I got the impression from our conversation yesterday you had something you wanted to talk to me about."

His question caught me by surprise, although by that time I should have become used to his bluntness. As usual, I found myself stumbling over my reply. "I—that is, I just wanted to thank you. For the gift, I mean. It was thoughtful." Once again, I felt the heat rushing to my face. It seemed that awkward embarrassment was to be a common state for me whenever I was around this man.

He smiled at me smugly. "Apparently, it doesn't take much to charm you. I can't imagine how grateful you would have been if I had sent you an entire six-pack of the stuff." He shifted in his seat and leaned closer to me. "Now. Why don't you tell me what this is really about?"

The waitress appeared at that moment with our orders, which gave me a precious few seconds to collect my wits while she placed our food on the table. Jon sat quietly staring at me while

I began to dig into my food. I hoped, if I filled my mouth, I could further delay answering his question. Unfortunately, all my attempt at gluttony gained me was the feeling that the food was stuck in my throat while I squirmed under his piercing gaze. Eventually, I was able to choke down the mouthful and took a sip of tea. "I'm interested in doing a story on your appointment to the Metropolitan Historical Commission, what your plans are, how you became interested in becoming a volunteer, that sort of thing. It's pretty unusual for a newcomer to be appointed to anything of that much local importance."

He picked up his spoon and scooped out a bite of chili before giving me a knowing look. "I see.

If I'm such an outsider, what possible interest could anyone have in my plans? Or is that just an excuse you've cooked up to see me again? Really Georgia, if you wanted to go out on a date with me, you could have just asked."

The level of this man's arrogance was immeasurable, and I found it difficult to sit still under his unnerving gaze. All I wanted to do was to run out the door and never think of Jon Barnett again. I was considering doing exactly that when I heard a familiar voice at my shoulder.

"Barnett, you old buzzard! How did you discover our secret club?"

Jon stood to shake Mayor Brill's hand. "Mr. Mayor. It seems I have stumbled into the right place. Are you telling me this is one of your regular haunts?"

An idea began to dawn on me as the two men traded barbs and clapped each other on the shoulder. Perhaps it hadn't been an accident that Jon chose this place to meet. After all, the mayor's fondness for the Varallo's chili was widely known. There had been cartoons created to suggest that the gaseous backfire of the chili beans had prompted some of his less popular political decisions. But why would Jon need an excuse to run into him, since the mayor had been instrumental in his appointment to the commission? It seemed there was more to their relationship than the obvious. Mayor Brill certainly seemed on especially friendly terms with Jon, if his initial greeting was any indication. The question I needed to find an answer to was how deep their friendship went. As these thoughts were churning in my mind, I became aware that both men were staring at me.

"I'm sorry. Did you say something to me?" I looked from one to the other.

Both men erupted in raucous laughter at my question. "So, this is the fireball female reporter you were telling me about?" The mayor addressed the question to Jon. "Can't say I understand what you were so worried about. She seems pretty tame to me."

Jon's face took on a dour expression and his previous good mood seemed to take a steep dive. He looked pointedly at the mayor. "Nice of you to stop by, Mr. Mayor. Perhaps we can meet soon to talk about that building renovation we were discussing. "

The mayor's face seemed to blanch slightly as if he realized he'd just spoken out of turn. "Yes. Let's do that. I'll have my secretary give you a call." He turned and looked down at me. "Nice to meet you, Miss Ayres." As he walked away, Jon took his seat at the table and began to dig into his bowl of chili as if he suddenly realized he was famished. When he finished, and pushed back from the table, I decided to take a chance at asking him a question.

"Now, I'm the one who's wondering what that was really all about. You and the mayor seemed to be pretty chummy. What building renovation were you referring to?"

His eyes took on the same dark and hooded look I remembered from our first meeting. "Be careful, Georgia. Don't ask questions unless you're prepared for the answers."

If his warning had the intended effect of shutting me up and preventing any further discussion, he was successful. We finished our meal in relative silence, only exchanging a few polite words to fill the awkwardness that descended over us after the mayor's departure. My lunch with Jon hadn't turned out at all like I planned. I felt I was no closer to finding answers to my questions than I had been the day before. It was even possible my stumbling attempts to dig for information may have pushed me even further away from the truth.

As our lunch date ended, Jon offered me a polite handshake and thanked me for my company. I watched him walk away, uncertain what had happened to cause his mood to shift so suddenly. His earlier warning to "be careful what I asked for" continued to nag at me. It reminded me of something, but I couldn't put my finger on what until I was on my way back to work. His words had been an almost exact repeat of what Ida Hood said when I left her office.

So, what did those two have in common? The more I thought about it, the more likely it seemed everything was connected: his appointment to the commission, Ida's reaction when I mentioned his name, the mayor's overt friendliness with someone he was supposed to have just met, even that he "just happened" to meet me at the Ball. Was that also by design? My head was beginning to spin with the possibilities my questions were stirring up. I knew I would have to eventually get down to the business of figuring out all of the pieces of this puzzle, but for now, I just wanted to push it all out of my mind.

Chapter 9

The next day, I decided I needed a sounding board; someone whom I could discuss ideas with who had no vested interest in the results of my ruminations other than to help me sort them out. That description fit Julie perfectly. She had a remarkable knack for wading through my verbal ramblings in a way that helped me get to the heart of what I was searching for. I gave her a call and we arranged to meet for dinner that night at *Rotier's*, a small family owned restaurant. Their claim to fame was a fantastic cheeseburger on French bread, served by a foul-mouthed waitress who could be counted on to treat both regulars and new customers to an entertaining shower of verbal abuse.

I arrived at the restaurant a little past six, and was seated in one of the forest green linoleum covered booths. There was a pretty good crowd already, and I was immediately greeted by the infamous waitress, Paula, who tossed a menu in front of me and warned me not to take all day deciding. Luckily, Julie arrived a few minutes later, and we placed our orders for cheeseburgers, fries, and two of their icy cold milkshakes served in metal mixer cups. While we were waiting, I launched into a description of my recent conversations with Jon Barnett, the peculiar coincidence of his encounter with the mayor, and the odd warning I received from both Jon and Ida Hood.

Paula brought our orders at the same time I reached the end of my monologue, and we both dove into the food. We shared a few mutual groans of delight as we stuffed our mouths full. Julie took a long sip of her milkshake and shook her head at me with a smile. "It sounds like Mr. Gorgeous has become Mr. Mysterious. You sure know how to pick 'em, girl."

I dipped a French fry into the ketchup I had poured on the plate and chewed thoughtfully. "Well, first off, I didn't pick him for anything. He just insinuated himself into my life, and I seem to be destined to keep running into him. But yes, he is mysterious. I was hoping you could help me figure out what he's up to."

She shrugged her shoulders as she considered what I said. "I think this guy is bad news waiting to happen. All69 the signs suggest he's up to something." She took another slurp of her milkshake and looked deep in thought. "What about trying to talk to Ida Hood again? Maybe she'd be willing to explain what she meant, because it sure sounds like she has some inside info on the guy."

I nodded my agreement. "I think you're right. But I'm not sure how to approach her. She seemed to pull back just when I thought she was about to tell me something important."

"You're a reporter, right? Use that. Tell her you want to write a story on some of the historic buildings that are targeted for renovation. Ask her to suggest which ones you should pick. If she's as passionate about it as you've described, she'll probably jump at the chance to point you in a certain direction. That should put you in a good place to talk to her about other things."

I considered her suggestion carefully. "Maybe. But she seems pretty sharp. Don't you think she might see right through me? If she thinks I'm being cagey, she might clam up even more."

Julie shrugged her shoulders. "Then use your judgment. Why not just go visit her again and see how things develop? I still think she's your best bet for figuring out what Barnett is up to."

I smiled at my friend. "Maybe you should be the reporter. You have such a good way of cutting to the chase. I always get myself twisted up in the 'what-ifs' and 'maybes'."

She laughed enthusiastically. "Can you just imagine what would happen if we were both reporters? We'd make ourselves crazy trying not to hurt each other's feelings by getting the most stories into print. No, thank you. I'm happy to stick to my job at the bank. That's where the money is, you know."

It was an old joke between us to suggest that working at a bank would result in her having more of the green stuff, too. Unfortunately, Julie's job as a teller paid only slightly more than mine, which was why we both considered eating burgers and fries at a restaurant to be a luxury.

We stood and went to the cash register to pay our separate checks, before heading out into the cool night air. I gave Julie a firm hug and thanked her for listening to me.

"Anytime. Someday I may need you to return the favor." She began to walk toward her car, then turned around once more. "Talk to her, Georgia." I nodded and thought to myself, *easier said than done*. But I knew she was right.

Chapter 10

Three weeks would pass before I was able to make good on my promise to Julie. Just when I thought I would be relegated to being a one-story reporter, I began to receive other assignments. My days suddenly became filled with following storylines and tracking down sources. I felt like a true newspaper reporter for the first time.

Most of the story leads I was assigned were profiles that focused on individuals in the Nashville community who had made, or were making, a name for themselves for their involvement in some notable event or activity. Attaching their profile to a newsworthy story was known in the industry as a *news peg*. Prior to conducting the interviews that led to these profiles, I was careful to prepare ahead with questions that would, hopefully, direct the discussion towards a particular topic which may otherwise be lost in a discussion of more mundane issues.

One of my favorite profiles involved a well-known local woman, Rosa Decavanta, who ran one of the most popular and successful clothing stores in the city. That was old news which wouldn't interest very many people, except perhaps those who were looking for a place to shop. I had no interest in writing a piece that described the vagaries of couture that one could find in her store. The real news had to do with her ties to a family from New Jersey suspected of being heavily involved in the American Mafia, otherwise known as the *Cosa Nostra*. Rosa was the only daughter of Antonio Decavanta. Rumor had it that she fled New Jersey after a scandal that led to the incarceration of her father and several other family members. From what I could gather from my interview with Rosa, she had no involvement with the illegal activities of the other members of her family. She just wanted to start a new and simple life for herself far away from New Jersey.

The story on Rosa was the last one I had been assigned. I was glad to finally be able to take a well-earned break after it had gone to print. My story also garnered the attention of Mr. Stein, who summoned me to his office once again. I knocked carefully on his door and he waved me in. To my surprise, he stood when I entered and held out his hand.

"Well done, Ayres. That piece on Rosa Decavanta was top notch."

I shook his hand and returned his smile. "Thank you. She made it easy. I think she really wanted the story to come out so she could clear her name."

He waved me to a seat as he sat in his own worn brown leather chair. "Sometimes we get lucky that way. Other times, following a lead is like pulling teeth with the subject moaning and groaning the entire time." I noticed the look on his face shifted from friendly to something I couldn't quite pinpoint. Could it be he looked a little nervous? "By the way. There's no need to keep digging around for a story on Barnett. I don't think there's anything there. It's best if you just drop it."

His suggestion surprised me more than a little. I wondered what could have caused him to change his mind so radically. I guess I was beginning to develop my reporter's gut because I decided the wisest course for me to take was to hold my tongue and agree with him. "Okay. If you think that's best," I replied.

A look of relief crossed his face. "Great, great. Now look. Why don't you take the rest of the day off? Go out and get some fresh air. You've done good work lately, and you deserve a breather."

Yes, his behavior was definitely strange. This wasn't the gruff *by the book* boss I was used to, but I sure wasn't going to question his offer. I thanked him and left his office. Yes, I led him to believe I was going to follow his advice and stop probing into Barnett's business. The truth was his uncharacteristic request only served to pique my interest even more. Apparently, something had happened to make Mr. Stein want to put me off the trail of Jon Barnett, but that didn't mean I had to follow his lead. In my mind, it only meant there was even more reason to find out exactly what was going on. That meant paying another visit to Ida Hood.

Chapter 11

My chance to follow-up on my plan came two days later when I was sent to do a story on a case being tried at the courthouse. When the trial ended for the day, I was able to walk the short distance to the Stahlman building, to once again knock on the door of the MHC office. I heard the sound of shuffling feet inside and the door opened to reveal Miss Hood. I wasn't sure how she would react to seeing me again, so I was pleasantly surprised when she greeted me warmly.

"Well look who's here." Her face lit up in a smile as she opened the door wider. "Come in. Come in. I've heard the most wonderful news today, and I've been wishing I had someone to share it with." She led me to where the two chairs were still positioned near the windows and gestured for me to sit. She perched on the edge of the other chair and regarded me with excitement. "You remember our discussion about my aunt? The one I'm named after?" I nodded. "Well, I had a call today from the mayor's office saying the Belmont Mansion, the original site of my aunt's school for women, has been placed on the National Register of Historic Places. That means funds will be pigeonholed for its restoration and preservation." She clapped her hands in delight. "It also means there will be a permanent museum to honor the story of my aunt and the other women who worked so hard to create a significant life for the young girls who would attend their schools."

Her joy was so palpable I couldn't help but share in her excitement. I reached forward and clasped her hands in mine. "That's wonderful news. I'm so happy for you and your family."

She squeezed my hands and shifted so she sat more fully on her chair. "Yes. It's what I've been hoping for, for a very long time. It's why I came back to Nashville; to see if I could find a way to keep alive the good work my aunt did. She left me a sizable amount of money in her will, and I've always had the idea of using it somehow to continue her dream. I finally realized that restoring the Mansion was the best way to accomplish that. Unfortunately, the estimates of what it would take to make that happen were far beyond her generous bequest. So, I set my hat on working for this Commission in order to make it happen. I was beginning to give up hope, especially after Mr. Barnett came to town."

Her last comment took me by surprise. I suddenly remembered the real reason I had come to see her. "The last time I was here, I got the impression you weren't very keen on him. I wanted to ask you why, but I was hesitant because you also said I should be careful about the questions I asked. I've been wondering what you meant?"

Her expression changed to a frown as she turned to stare out the window. "Sometimes I say things I shouldn't. It's a habit that comes from spending too much time in my own company. I'm so used to speaking out loud to myself, I sometimes forget someone else may be listening." She turned her eyes back to regard me. "I knew of Jon Barnett before he came to Nashville. I spent some time living in Washington, D.C. a few years back, and there was quite a bit of talk there about his family's activities. You knew they were involved in buying up newspapers?"

I nodded in response to her question. "I heard that. In fact, his arrival in Nashville gave my editor more than a little cause to worry."

"And rightly so," she replied. It's my understanding he came here to make some big acquisition. When he was appointed to the commission, I was sure it must mean he was going to appropriate the rights to purchase some of our historical buildings before they were protected; perhaps turn one into a publishing house for some of the newspapers his family owns here in the South. He came to this office one day asking a lot of questions about the Belmont Mansion. I tried to put him off the scent by telling him how old and run down it was. That it was just full of drafts and in need of extensive work. Of course, that's all true, but I did try to embellish the facts a bit. I've been holding my breath until that call came in today."

Well, that explained at least part of the puzzle I had been wrestling with. It made sense that being on the Historical Commission would enable him to have a front row seat to observe every transaction that involved some of the most prime real estate property in the city. What wasn't clear was what the mayor had to do with his whole scheme. Mayor Brill was a member of the Democratic Party, but he was a conservative member, at best. There was no question, when it came to news coverage of his activities, *The Daily Courier* took a less favorable stance than *The Nashville News*. Not surprising, given they were each firmly planted in opposite political arenas. In fact, sometimes the dual reporting of the Nashville political scene by the two newspapers had the atmosphere of a rooster fight with neither party emerging from the battle unscathed.

I must have been silent for too long while these thoughts were whirling through my brain, because I looked up to find Miss Hood studying me closely. She leaned toward me and placed her hand on my knee. "You looked like you were lost in thought. Do you want to tell me what's worrying you?"

I was considering whether or not to reveal my concerns to her when the door burst open, spilling Jon Barnett into the room. His face was unsmiling as he looked from Miss Hood to me. "Georgia." He nodded at me. "I guess I shouldn't be surprised to find you here, since you seem to keep turning up when I least expect it. But I have to admit, I'm rather shocked to find you in this particular office." His glance shifted from me to Miss Hood and back again, as if he was waiting for one of us to offer an explanation. To my relief, Miss Hood spoke first.

"Miss Ayres has been interviewing me for a story she's going to write on the restoration of the Belmont Mansion and my family's role in its history. We met a while back, and I thought of her immediately when I received the call from the mayor's office informing me it was to be listed on the National Register." Her back straightened with pride as she spoke. "What we'd both like to know, I'm sure, is why *you* are here?"

I had to struggle to avoid smiling at how easily she had turned the tables on him, which, in my experience, was not an easy feat, given how smug and over-confidant he always appeared to be. For a second, he seemed at a loss for words.

"Actually, I came to see you." His voice projected a tone of friendliness, even while his eyes bore into Miss Hood with a barely contained threat. "Mayor Brill told me of the decision about the Mansion. I came to offer my congratulations."

Miss Hood's face betrayed her distrust in his explanation. "Humph. I hardly think that's likely, since you've made little effort to hide your own intentions toward the place from the start. Why don't you tell us why you're really here? Perhaps you've set your sights on some other historical morsel?"

The scene playing out in front of me had me speechless with wonder. Jon had the size advantage over Miss Hood, since he stood a good ten inches taller and weighed at least seventy-five pounds more. But whatever had sparked her into action was filling her with such a fierce power she seemed to grow in size as I watched. He stood staring down at her in a none-to-subtle effort at intimidation, his eyes flashing darkly in his unblinking gaze, while she remained seated with a look of calm determination. Finally, he turned and trailed out the door as rapidly as he had entered. Miss Hood and I looked at each other and let out a simultaneous *whew*.

"Lord, that felt good," she said. Her face was stretched into a huge grin. "I feel like I just won the grand prize at the county fair."

I laughed out loud at the image. "You're so brave. I wish I had one-tenth of your spunk."

Miss Hood's face showed her pleasure. "There's something to be said for growing old. You tend to be less intimidated by things that used to scare the woolies out of you. But here's a bit of wisdom I can share with you, my dear. Our former first lady, Eleanor Roosevelt, a woman I admire very much, once said, "No one can make you feel intimidated without your consent". Whenever I find myself in a situation where I feel I'm being bullied, and that encounter with Jon Barnett definitely fits that description, I try to focus on those words. They have never failed to give me strength, in even the most trying of circumstances."

I reflected upon what she said. I suppose it is true that you have to allow someone to intimidate you, or scare you, or belittle you in order for it to happen. Otherwise, they're just throwing empty words in your direction. Unfortunately, I had allowed myself to be the target of those attacks my entire life. I was only now realizing I could choose to step out of their path.

"Maybe one day I'll be able to have your strength when I'm in a similar situation. I have to admit that I was scared to death watching the two of you face off with each other."

She smiled reassuringly. "You're stronger than you realize, my dear. We all are. We just have to get out of our own way sometimes." She patted me on the knee. "Jon Barnett is not really the brute he likes to pretend to be. He's just playing the role he's been taught to play his whole life. I imagine a lot of his bravado is designed to cover-up his discomfort with having to always be the one in control. It must be awfully tiring to never be able to show vulnerability."

Her words were indeed reassuring. I was again reminded of my grandmother who had never failed to bolster my self-confidence in circumstances which felt to a young child like the most terrible thing that could ever happen. Well, I wasn't a young child anymore. It was time I started allowing myself to become the kind of woman I wanted to be. Miss Hood helped me realize that what kind of person I chose to be, and whom I chose to become, was up to me. Now I just had to figure out what that was.

Chapter 12

I decided to actually write the story Miss Hood had fabricated for Jon Barnett's sake. It was printed on the front page of the local news section and included a photograph of her standing in front of the Belmont Mansion holding a framed picture of her aunt and the other teacher who founded the first school. The article gained me praise from my boss, Don Williams, as well as a few begrudged words of congratulations from my co-workers. I felt I was at last on my way professionally. Assignments were now coming to me regularly, and I was no longer relegated to the position of gopher among the staff. That role had fallen to the newest copy boy. Like I had been, he was fresh out of high school, and as untrained as a newborn puppy. He even looked a little like one as he zipped around the newsroom with a goofy grin on his face, inevitably crashing into someone who happened to step into his path.

One of the advantages of having more work to do was that I had managed to put Jon Barnett out of my thoughts. That's what I told myself, though I wasn't far from thinking of him quite often. There was a popular saying that *no news is good news*. That might be true in many of life's circumstances, but the opposite was true in the newspaper business. Whenever there was a paucity of news about some event or person, we had a lead on, it meant that something was likely brewing beneath the calm, misleading surface. I didn't really know what was obvious about Jon Barnett, other than he was irritating, smug, arrogant, self-assured, and never failed to simultaneously fluster and embarrass me. Then there were his eyes. Oh Lord, those eyes. Every time I looked at him, I became lost in those dark pools of light, suddenly unable to form a clear thought.

Miss Hood said he wasn't a bad guy... "wasn't a brute", was how she had put it. How he acted was just a reflection of his upbringing. I didn't find that very reassuring, since the same could be said of every one of us. *Oh, you're a serial killer? Well, that's just a reflection of your upbringing!* At what point do we draw the line on blaming the past? I knew my tendency for self-deprecation and reticence reflected a childhood plagued with criticism and distancing by my parents. It was a tough childhood in some ways, but I didn't believe that gave me the right to wallow in self-pity. All any of us could do about the past was to learn from it. We had the choice to either use what we learned to give us a leg up on understanding ourselves, or allow it to hold us in one place, where we continuously replayed the recorded loop of our past experiences.

My tendency was usually to take the latter approach, which involved me tormenting myself with a boundless litany of self-aggrandizing tapes of what I could have done, or should have done, or should or shouldn't have said in any given situation. I suppose that's why my cat was the love of my life. As long as I fed her on a regular basis, and gave her a warm lap to snuggle in from time to time, she regarded me with unveiled adoration. People's feelings were harder to discern. I usually assumed the worst whenever I was faced with trying to understand them.

That's also why Julie and I had been best friends since our freshman year in high school. I first met her when I was sitting alone at a table in our school cafeteria on my third day as a freshman. I was attempting to appear nonchalant in my obvious isolation from any social circles. I was yet to even comprehend, much less be invited, to join. I attended an all-girls school where cliques were as prominent as social sororities in most colleges. The two groups that held the most power at my school were composed of what I called the "popular girls" and the "artsy types". I hadn't grown up with the popular girls, which was a requirement in order to be admitted into their ranks. I wasn't as quirky as the artsy types, who wore their peculiarity like a badge of honor. That left the rest of us to sort ourselves out into some sort of social strata. On day three, I still hadn't managed to figure out where I might fit, so I claimed a seat in the most remote corner of the cafeteria, in an attempt to avoid notice. It felt like grade school all over again.

Every day, I would slip into the cafeteria carrying my brown paper lunch bag and school work, stop to buy a carton of milk from the food line, then briskly make my way to my table where I spent the next half hour peering down at one of my textbooks. My hope was that I looked studious. My fear was that I looked pitiful.

Three days into my self-imposed exile, I was rescued from what could have become a permanent fate by a tap on the shoulder. I turned to see a rather petite girl standing behind me with a friendly smile and the prettiest blue eyes I had ever seen. Unfortunately, they were hidden behind the largest pair of heavy tortoise shell glasses I had also ever seen. They were so big they gave the impression of hubcaps, because they reached all the way to her cheekbones on the sides, covered her eyebrows on the top, and dipped down close to her chin at the bottom. They kept slipping down her nose, too, causing her to constantly push them back up with one finger. The overall effect was both comical and sad.

"Mind if I sit here?" She asked, plopping her lunch tray and stack of books on the table across from me without waiting for a reply. "I've seen you sitting here by yourself the past few days and I thought you might like company. The truth is, I wanted company, and I thought you might not mind if I joined you." She took a hearty bite of her sandwich before continuing to speak. "I just transferred here from Cincinnati. I thought Southerners were supposed to be super friendly, but boy, this bunch is a tough nut to crack.

I was so shocked by her sudden appearance and continuous monologue, delivered at the same time she robustly consumed a lunch large enough to satisfy two football players, that I barely noticed when she stopped speaking. I blushed in embarrassment when I realized she was staring at me.

"I'm sorry. Did you ask me a question?" I asked.

"No. I was just wondering what you were thinking. My name's Julie."

"I'm Georgia. Do you always eat that much?"

She giggled. "I'm afraid so. I come from a long line of big eaters. Fortunately, we also have the metabolism of hummingbirds, so it doesn't really stay put." She gestured at her slim frame. "I wouldn't mind putting on a few pounds. It might make me a little more successful in the boy department." She gazed at me curiously. "Are you from around here?"

I felt my face flush again. It was a tiresome reaction, but one I found impossible to control. It seemed whenever I felt the least bit uncomfortable, my face would betray my feelings before my mouth could form a reply. In this case, my discomfort stemmed from my impression that she viewed my solitary lunch habit as the result of my status as an out-of-towner, like herself. I was embarrassed to tell her that I had lived my entire life in Nashville, which could only suggest I was alone because no one wanted to sit with me. To my surprise, she seemed to read my thoughts without me saying a word, a trait I found endearing, and would eventually help to cement our friendship for the rest of our lives. To state it simply, Julie was very perceptive, but she was also kind in her proffered interpretation of what she perceived. In this instance, she quickly answered her own question, which rescued me from the humiliation of explaining things myself.

"But of course, you're from here," She said with a wave of her hand. "That's why you're so comfortable doing your own thing instead of feeling like you have to be a crowd pleaser." She finished her lunch and curiously eyed the remains of my lunch bag. "Are you going to eat that cookie?" She had her gaze fixed on a rather large chocolate chip cookie my mother had snuck into my lunch bag that morning. My dad had warned me on more than one occasion to watch what I ate, because, in his words, I wouldn't "be built like a scarecrow forever". He went on to explain that I had my mother's genes and I'd better watch it or I would end up fat. My mother tended to be on the plump side, and my dad was constantly nagging her to lose weight. I don't think his reproves were working. I frequently spotted evidence of her secret rebellion in the form of empty candy wrappers tucked behind the Kotex box in the bathroom, or half empty bags of cookies stashed behind the cereal boxes in the kitchen cupboard. She knew my dad was unlikely to spot them in either place because he wouldn't be caught dead anywhere near *ladies' products*, as he called them. God forbid he ever did so much as fill a bowl of cereal to feed himself.

Sweets were her comfort. I wondered if slipping one into my lunch bag was her way of showing love, or maybe it was just her way of sharing her guilt. Neither of my parents were inclined to show outward signs of affection, but were masters at handing out guilt. I had grown used to expecting that any attention I received from them was to point out something they were disappointed about. The idea that her including a cookie in my lunch was just one item in a long list of rebukes made me grab the cookie and toss it to Julie a little more forcefully than I meant to, causing it to break into several pieces.

"Whoa! What brought that on?" She looked down at the broken cookie, then up at me with a look of amazed shock.

"I'm sorry. I shouldn't have thrown it at you. It just reminded me of something unpleasant."

She shrugged and began to fill her mouth with the broken pieces. "That's okay," she said between bites, "we all have our days."

I was relieved to see my first possible friend at school hadn't fled at my crazed reaction. It was right then I swore a silent vow of perpetual allegiance to this odd and amazing girl.

Julie and I became fast friends. Over time, her huge eyeglasses had been replaced by contact lens, which allowed her beauty to emerge like a monarch butterfly from the chrysalis that kept it hidden from sight. The change created such a sudden transformation in her looks that she began to attract quite a bevy of admirers from the flock of local boys who hung around our school after hours. It also garnered her the attention of the popular girls, who likely felt it was safer to keep her close, than wonder if the male object of their own attention was shifting his focus to her. Julie, bless her heart, was oblivious to all of it, preferring instead to hang out with me and a steadily growing group of girls who either did not, or chose not, to fit in with the more exclusive circles.

Over the years, Julie's beauty continued to blossom, but she remained just as unaffected by the attention it brought her as she was in high school. I, on the other hand, had just begun to "come into my looks" during the past couple of years. My body had finally filled out in all the right places, but I still struggled to overcome the image of myself as the gangly wallflower who was always passed up at the school dances. Perhaps that was why being around Jon Barnett bothered me so much. He reminded me of all the gorgeous, swaggering, unreachable boys who regarded me as unworthy of their attention, when they bothered to notice me at all.

I was determined not to be that girl anymore. Instead, I wanted to have the confidence of Eleanor Roosevelt, and the courage of Ida Hood. I wanted to be a person who was worthy of the attention of someone as handsome as Jon Barnett, although now I realized I also wanted to find out if he was worthy of me. I needed to know what he was up to, and in the process, uncover the truth about why he was in Nashville.

Chapter 13

I didn't have to wait long to find my answers. I had been invited to attend a dinner party the following Saturday night, hosted by Ralph Stein and his wife. Actually, everyone on the staff of *The Nashville News* had been invited, from the lowest copy boy to the section editors. There was an air of crackling excitement around the newsroom for the entire week leading up to the event, since it would be the first time most of us had been the recipients of such an invitation. The dinner was to be held at *Cheekwood*, a former lavish country house estate that was now the site of a museum and botanical gardens. I actually wrote a feature article on the history of *Cheekwood* for my high school paper, and I dug it out to refresh my memory of its history. The Cheeks were one of Nashville's first true entrepreneurial families. In the late 1800s, two cousins named Christopher and Joel Cheek established the Nashville Coffee and Manufacturing Company. The company became famous for marketing a roasted, blended coffee at a time when other companies sold only green coffee beans.

Over the next few years, the Cheeks formed a partnership with James Neal and expanded their coffee production business across the country, under the name of Cheek-Neal Coffee. They also convinced the *Maxwell House Hotel*, which at the time was considered the finest hotel in Nashville, to use their coffee exclusively. Eventually, they acquired the use of the hotel's name for marketing the coffee. According to historical reports, the coffee's fame soared largely as a result of a visit to the hotel by President Theodore Roosevelt, who claimed the coffee was "good to the last drop". This later became the slogan that branded the coffee. Sales of the company to *Postum*, then to *General Foods*, provided the fortune that eventually led to the design, architecture, furnishings, and landscaping of *Cheekwood*, whose name combines that of Leslie Cheek, son of Christopher, with that of his wife Mabel Wood.

As part of my research for my article, I spent several hours roaming the main house and grounds of *Cheekwood*. The grandeur, prevalent during the early years of its existence, was still very much in evidence in modern times. I suspected the dinner party would be quite a fete. In fact, the invitation stated that formal attire was required. Since there was nothing in my wardrobe that could pass for formal, with the exception of the old prom dress, I decided a shopping trip would be necessary. Luckily, Julie agreed to accompany me on the mission. I didn't really have a clue what would be considered appropriate, other than it needed to be floor length and look classier than anything I had ever worn. Julie was more experienced at picking this sort of attire, since her work at the bank allowed her to attend formal events with some regularity. It wasn't that tellers were often called upon to be available for such occasions, but she had been dating Harry, the branch manager, for over a year. Regular formal dinners had become part of her social life.

Julie suggested we check out the dress selection at the *Cain-Sloan* department store. It was located downtown on Church Street, and since her bank was just down the street from the store, we decided to meet there after work. When I arrived at the store, I took the escalator up to the third floor where the women's fine dresses were located and found Julie already engrossed in selecting several possible choices from a rack of formal gowns. A saleswoman stood at her side to collect the dresses and, I imagined, make sure they were handled with care. My stomach clenched when I realized I would have to try them on. For some reason, I had ignored that fact. I assumed I could just point and pick one from the proffered selections. I hated viewing myself in the unforgiving neon light of dressing rooms. Whoever thought seeing oneself displayed in such a way would actually encourage purchasing the items, knew nothing about how women think. Had the room been bathed in a warm glow designed to soften imperfections and lend a romantic haze to the image it would have been more effective in encouraging sales. Instead, I always found the prospect of entering a dressing room akin to being told to undress to put on a gown for a doctor's examination; both left me feeling terribly exposed!

Just as I was wondering if I could backtrack down the escalator without being seen, Julie spotted me. "You're here! Come see what I've found. They have some wonderful choices, and there's a sale going on. too!"

She obviously had a lot more enthusiasm for this outing than I did. I smiled uncertainly at the dresses she held up. "Are you sure we can't just pick one and see how it fits once I get home?"

She shook her head determinedly. "No, silly. That would be a waste of time. Besides, don't you want to see which one looks best on you?"

I was about to comment on how I doubted *any* of them would look on me the way she envisioned, when the saleswoman stepped forward. "Why don't I show you to a dressing room? You can try on a few to start with, and if you don't find one to your liking, we'll just keep bringing more until you do." She smiled at me warmly. I suspected she was used to dealing with reluctant shoppers like myself, and she had perfected the fine art of coaxing a sale out of even the most hesitant.

Reluctantly, I allowed her to lead me into a dressing room and pulled the curtain shut behind me. I examined the four gowns that had been left for me, quickly ruling out two of the four that appeared too elaborately embellished for my taste. A third seemed a possibility. It was a purplish color with thin shoulder straps and a sort of gathering across the front that I hoped might give a little more shape to my rather modest bosom. I set it aside and held up the fourth selection. It was pale turquoise blue made out of soft material, with cap sleeves adorned with silver beads that extended down the sides of the bodice and across the middle, giving the impression of a belt around the waist. The bottom of the gown hung in soft folds to the floor. The back was partially exposed and dipped down to a V-shaped area of crisscrossed ribbons.

The material was light, loose, and shifted easily when I swung the gown from side to side. I actually found myself excited to try it on. When I pulled it over my head and chanced a look into the mirror, my breath caught at the image. *Could that be me?* The blue and silver seemed to send a shimmer of light that reflected off my light brown hair, and the snug bodice that topped the loosely hung layers below gave the impression of curves where I knew there were hardly any. I pushed the curtain aside and stepped into the outer area where Julie and the salesperson were waiting.

The salesperson stepped forward and straightened the gown slightly. "Your friend is right. This is a wonderful color for you, and the style suits you perfectly. We just need to find some shoes that will match and a couple of other accessories."

I glanced at my bare feet and giggled. "Yeah, I suppose my sneakers won't work with this dress. But do you think you can find something that won't make my feet hurt all night?" I was remembering my last unpleasant experience with the heels I had worn at the Belle Meade Mansion Ball.

The salesperson nodded with a smile. "I think we can manage to find something that will work." As she walked away, I looked at Julie who was dabbing at her eyes with a tissue.

"Is it that much of a shock?" I asked.

"Oh no! Not at all! It's just that you look so wonderful." She walked over to me and put her hand on my arm. "You always seem so reluctant to try something new, as if you're expecting it to turn out disastrous. I've always felt so bad to see you go through that struggle every time you considered opening up to life a little bit. To see you like this, to see the courage it took to allow yourself to even step out of that dressing room, well, it just makes me so happy for you."

I felt uncomfortable being the object of so much attention, and I suddenly couldn't wait to get out of the dress. "Okay. Now you're just making me feel weird. Why don't I take off this get-up and we hit the *Iris Room* for their soup and sandwich special of the day. Trying on clothes has worked up my appetite."

Julie wisely chose not to comment on my obvious attempt to change the subject, and I was silently grateful to her for that. While I was changing, she collected the shoes, handbag, and shawl the salesperson selected and waited for me at the cash register. When I saw the sales receipt, I had a flash of panic, since it totaled almost more than I earned in a week. I decided to ignore the alarm going off in my head and just fork over the cash before I changed my mind.

Fifteen minutes later, we were seated in the Iris Room with my purchases stacked beside me. Julie glanced over at me with a knowing look. "I know what you're thinking. You're wondering if you can get out of this dinner and sneak back to return all these things."

I looked at her with wonder. "How do you do that? Do you have some sort of secret powers that allow you to read my mind?"

She smiled like the Cheshire cat in Alice in Wonderland. "I have many secret powers, not the least of which is reading your mind. But honestly, you have one of those faces that always give away what you're thinking. Let's just say you should never consider becoming a poker player."

I waggled my head at her and studied the menu. "Good thing I don't plan to! By the way, lunch is on you."

She laughed and opened her menu. "If that's what it takes to get you to wear that dress, I'll gladly pay for your lunch every day for a week. Of course, you'd have to settle for tea and crackers. I'm afraid my budget wouldn't allow for much more."

We both fell into a comfortable silence as we scanned the menu and made our choices. I felt an unfamiliar sense of calm that I could only attribute to facing one of my greatest fears and succeeding. I remembered reading somewhere that "courage was not the absence of fear but just deciding to act in spite of it". That's how I felt about purchasing the gown, and preparing to go to the formal dinner. I was still plagued by the fear that I would appear like a child playing dress-up, but I was determined to push through my apprehension and be open to the experience. To my surprise, once I made that decision, the worries that always seemed to be my constant companions began to dissipate. I found that I was actually beginning to look forward to the dinner.

Chapter 14

On the night of the dinner, I pulled into the drive that led to the *Cheekwood* mansion and found myself in a long line of cars waiting to be attended by several young men hired to serve as valets. When my turn came, I handed over the keys to *Tweedledee* and allowed the valet to help me from the car. The night was unseasonably mild for mid-February, so I loosely draped my new shawl over my shoulders as I looked down to appraise the condition of my dress. I was relieved to see that even being crumpled up in the tight space of my Bug had not managed to mar its appearance. I took a deep breath to calm my nerves and headed into the mansion.

Once inside, we were directed up a flight of stairs to the second floor where tables had been set up on the loggia. The room was warmly lit by hundreds of candles placed throughout the area. Subtle strains of music were wafting in from open, louvered doors leading out onto a stone terrace. Waiters roamed the area offering glasses of champagne carefully balanced on round trays. I accepted a glass from a nearby tray and took a small sip. To my surprise, the taste was pleasant, reminding me of a lighter and bubblier version of ginger ale.

I took a more generous swallow of champagne and scanned the room. The crowd was composed mostly of my co-workers from *The Nashville News*. They were accompanied by women I assumed must be their wives or girlfriends who I was relieved to see were dressed in outfits very similar to my own. Ralph Stein was standing off to one side in a small circle of guests. A woman I recognized as his wife stood beside him, and both of them were directing their attention to the Mayor, who was the guest of honor for the evening. Mayor Brill had been recently re-elected to his office, and I was sure that Mr. Stein was using the dinner as an opportunity to both congratulate him on his achievement and garner his good will toward the newspaper.

The combination of the crowd and the champagne began to make me feel a little too warm, so I wandered down the hallway to a second room which opened onto a small terrace covered by an arbor draped with wisteria vines. There were no blooms on the vines, which I suspected had to do with the time of the year. The pattern they created made the terrace appear to be swathed in a crisscrossed canopy allowing the twinkle of the stars overhead to peak through. The night air felt delicious on my bare arms, so I removed my shawl and laid it over the railing at the end of the terrace. The terrace overlooked the south gardens, which were illuminated by the careful placement of numerous lanterns. I knew the Harpeth hills rose just beyond the gardens, and I could just make out their shape in the shadowy distance.

"Beautiful, isn't it?"

There was no mistaking that voice. I should have realized he would be here. My heart felt like it was suddenly in my throat and my body seemed to have frozen in place.

"Though not as beautiful as the woman standing in front of me." I felt him move closer, as I struggled to catch my breath. "How are you, Georgia?"

I placed a hand on the railing to steady myself and slowly turned to face him. "Hello, Mr. Barnett. I'm surprised to see you here."

He smiled. "I thought we'd agreed you would call me Jon." He walked a few steps forward and leaned his body against the railing, allowing his hand to casually graze my arm. "It seems we both have a knack for surprising each other. I wasn't sure what kind of reception I'd receive from you after our last encounter."

The last time I saw him was when he had barged in and out of the MHC office, leaving a trail of smoldering anger in his wake. This seemed to be a common pattern to our meetings; unexpected encounters, hints of mystery, flashes of anger, and sudden departures. Overall, it made my head spin and my stomach tense, but there was also something about the combination that made me want to experience it again. I told myself it was just a physical spark that drew me back to this man, but the truth was probably more complex than that. It was almost as if I believed that by unraveling the mysteries surrounding him, I would be able to understand something elusive about myself.

"You have a way of stirring things up," I said. "I'm never quite sure what to expect from you."

This comment seemed to please him, "Isn't that a good thing? Not to be predictable? I find consistency to be overrated. It's too safe. The thing that exhilarates us, that gets our hearts pumping each day, is the challenge of exploring the unfamiliar. That's what gives purpose to our lives. Of course, the chance we take in living that way is that we might be disappointed with what we find. All we can do is decide if we're willing to risk everything in order to possibly find something rare and precious." His eyes seemed to study me closely for a moment. "Tell me Georgia, are you worth the risk?"

It was the longest speech I'd ever heard him give. I couldn't help but wonder if he had rehearsed it ahead of time. I found myself baffled by his question. Not only was I unsure how to answer, I was even less sure what it meant. Luckily, I was saved from having to blunder my way through a response as the tinkling of a bell signaled the start of dinner.

Jon looked up impatiently. "We'll have to resume this conversation later. The Mayor will be expecting me to join him. Will you wait for me after dinner?"

I nodded my head and allowed him to escort me into the loggia. There was a place card in front of every chair at the various tables, and after helping me locate my designated seat, he left to walk to the front of the room to take his own place next to the mayor. I was seated beside the new copy boy, who fingered his collar nervously while nodding to a steady stream of chatter from a heavily bejeweled woman on his right. An attractive blonde woman sat to my left; her face glued to a man on her other side. *At least I won't have to worry about making conversation,* I thought.

The dinner was served in multiple courses, each more enticing and delectable than the previous. After my unexpected and typically confusing encounter with Jon, I thought I would have lost my appetite, but the aromas filling the room had my mouth watering.

A menu describing the dishes had been placed across each plate that described the various dishes. The first course was a small pastry filled with creamy mushrooms in a delicate, flaky tart, accompanied by more sparkling champagne. It was followed by a salad of tender baby lettuce leaves, topped with sliced pears and slivered almonds in sweet-tangy dressing. The main dish consisted of slices of herb-crusted pork tenderloin that glistened from a coating of butter sauce, accompanied by roasted asparagus and baby new potatoes.

The champagne was replaced by a crisp white wine with the arrival of the salad course. The combination of free-flowing alcohol and delicious food appeared to have loosened the tongues of the guests, judging from the laughter, lively conversation, and groans of pleasure.

I stole what I hoped were discrete glances in Jon's direction, and was a little disappointed to always find him deep in conversation with either the Mayor, to his left, or an attractive, white-haired woman seated to his right. Although there was an obvious age disparity between them, I didn't doubt for a minute she was as enchanted by him as every other woman I had witnessed being the object of his attention. When I found myself considering walking up to him so that I could find out what he meant by his earlier comments, I carefully pushed my glass of wine out of reach.

As the plates were being cleared for the dessert course, I heard the tinkling of someone tapping a knife against one of the crystal glasses. I saw Mr. Stein standing at the main table, waiting for the crowd to quiet down. The noise in the room came to a standstill, except for the subtle clattering of forks on plates as some of the guests hurried to finish their entrees before they were removed.

As all eyes turned to the head table, Mr. Stein began to speak. "I'd like to welcome all of you here tonight and thank you for helping me congratulate Mayor Brill on his recent re-election. Please raise your glasses, and join me in a toast." There was the sound of shuffling as the guests lifted their glasses in unison. "To Mayor Brill, one of the most industrious mayors our city has ever had. Here's to another four, fruitful years."

The room was filled with shouts of "here, here," and glasses clinking in toasts. Mr. Stein raised his glass in the Mayor's direction and with a wave of a hand invited him to stand. The room erupted in applause as the mayor stood next to Mr. Stein and shook his hand. Several of the staff photographers, who had most likely been tipped off to expect such a scene, began flashing shots of the two men. The mayor placed an arm across Mr. Stein's shoulders, as they held the handshake and beamed at the cameras until the photo session ended. Then Mr. Stein stepped away and made a gesture to indicate that the mayor should address the crowd.

"Thank you, Ralph. It has always been my pleasure to be in such fine company as the men and women gathered here. I'm flattered to be your guest of honor. As many of you know, the newspaper business has a long and interesting history in this city that has, at times, been rather volatile, given the disparate political views embraced by our two representative papers." A few chuckles and murmurs of agreement could be heard throughout the room. "As you also know, I tend to lean more to one side than the other, although oftentimes my compatriots in the mayor's office would have liked to have seen me lean a little more heavily than I did." Laughter erupted in response to his comment. It was well known that although Mayor Brill's political stance was more representative of the Democratic than the Republican Party's viewpoints, his tendency to take a more conservative position on many key issues actually placed him more in the middle of the two. This had been a frequent bone of contention between the Mayor and other more democratically liberal politicians. It made the reporting of his activities particularly difficult for *The Nashville News,* known for its left-wing political leanings.

"I am pleased to announce to you today, that I have taken action that will partially remedy this disparity, at least when it comes to the printed version of the political activities of our local representatives of these two parties. As of yesterday, *The Daily Courier* became the property of the Barnett Corporation." The murmured sounds of shock and confusion filled the air. "I would now like to ask Jon Barnett, who is here to represent the corporation, to give us a brief description of what is planned for *The Daily Courier* from this point forward."

I could feel my mouth hanging open at the mayor's unexpected announcement. I watched with a mixture of anticipation and bewilderment as Jon rose to take the mayor's place. He stood quietly for a moment, letting the crowd noise subside as he scanned the large room. His eyes seemed to pause as they connected with mine, but I couldn't be certain.

"As many of you are aware, my family has been involved in the newspaper publishing business for many years. It has been our goal to acquire struggling but commendable papers in order to help them regain viability. I came to Nashville several months ago in order to discuss purchasing *The Daily Courier* from the Stahlman family. My intent was to identify new physical headquarters for the entire staff and equipment in order to allow the paper to continue publication. Unfortunately, the physical locations best suited for such an endeavor were either unavailable or designated for some other purpose. After much deliberation, and with the mayor's guidance, we have decided to discontinue publication of *The Daily Courier*. Of course, we will do everything possible to assist the existing staff with securing positions on other papers. Therefore, as of May 1st, *The Nashville News* will become the sole newspaper in Nashville."

His news was met with a cacophony of applause, exclamations, and rumblings as we all attempted to digest what he said. It was true that the diverse political views of the two papers had created more than a little discord in both the physical building where we were both housed, and in the city as the residents were drawn toward one side or the other. Nonetheless, there was a certain amount of vibrancy associated with the batting around of different viewpoints. It contributed to an atmosphere of what I thought of as *enthusiastic agitation*. I doubt any of us would have wished to see the paper go under, and we certainly did not sit comfortably with the knowledge that an entire staff could be terminated with the fell swoop of a moneyed corporation's fist.

As I looked around at the bewildered and anxious looks on my co-workers faces, I also began to sense the puzzle pieces start to fall into place. Jon's friendliness with the mayor, his appointment to the Historical Commission housed in a building owned by the Stahlman family, his anger upon learning the Belmont Mansion had been given protective status as a historical treasure, and perhaps even his showing up at the Ball where we first met, seemed to be part of a grand plan.

I tried to work through the facts as they had been presented, and a couple of things began to come together. The first was that the Mayor must have been supporting Jon's efforts, because they would help pave the way for the next stage of his political career. With *The Daily Courier* out of the way, the most evident opposition to his mayoral platform would be silenced. Second, Jon's appointment to the MHC afforded him the opportunity to not only cozy up to the Stahlman family, but to also have first-hand access to the choicest properties that might provide space for *The Daily Courier*. Apparently, the Belmont Mansion had been at the top of his list, until that plan fell through. What I couldn't understand was why the Mayor allowed the Mansion to be pushed off the negotiation table by his decision to designate it as a historical treasure. Unless that is, the Mayor stood to gain a lot more from *The Daily Courier's* closing than he would if it had just been relocated.

It suddenly dawned on me; that was why Jon had been so angry the day he showed up at the MHC office. He had no idea of what the mayor's plans were until the decision had been signed, sealed, and delivered to Ida Hood. By the time he learned of it, it must have been too late for him to cancel the deal he made with the Stahlmans to buy *The Daily Courier*. The question I couldn't figure out was; why didn't he just hold out for another location instead of shutting down the paper entirely? From what little I knew about his family's business dealings, buying a newspaper just to close it down seemed inconsistent with their usual mode of operating. Certainly counterproductive, from a strictly monetary point of view.

I was so lost in my thoughts I hadn't noticed that Jon was no longer standing at the front of the room. In fact, he seemed to have totally disappeared. I tried to act nonchalant as I picked at the slice of chocolate cake in front of me. After what felt like a lifetime, people finally began to push back their chairs and get up from the tables. I practically bolted from my seat and left the loggia. I hurried to the terrace where we met earlier that evening in hopes he might be waiting there, but unfortunately, he was nowhere in sight. I backtracked into the loggia in case he had returned, but also came up empty. Finally, in frustration, I made my way out the louvered doors onto the stone terrace in hopes of escaping the assorted guests who kept trying to engage me in conversation.

I walked quickly to the far edge of the patio and took a deep breath, letting the outward exhalation pull some of the tension from my chest. As my eyes adjusted to the dim light, I saw what appeared to be a flash of white in the shadows of the bushes bordering the lawn just beyond the edge of the patio. As I continued to gaze at the spot, the unmistakable image of the man I had been searching for came into view. I walked quickly toward him.

"Jon. I've been looking for you." Even in the dim light, I could make out the stern look on his face.

"Hello, Georgia. It seems my little announcement hasn't made me the most popular guy here tonight. Funny. I would have thought all of you would be thrilled to have less competition."

He seemed so morose I wanted to reach out to him, but something held me back. I still had questions to which I needed answers. Until I had them, I knew the wisest thing for me to do would be to keep my distance. "I suspect most people are wondering why you did it. Why you decided to buy *The Daily Courier* if you just intended to shut it down. Newspaper people are a tight bunch, even when we don't agree. We don't like to see some of our own get a raw deal. It makes us feel that we're vulnerable to the same fate."

He looked at me intently. "Is that what you think? That I just wanted to shut the paper down? Believe me, that's the last thing I wanted to happen."

"Then why? Why not stop it? Surely there's another option."

He shook his head slowly. "Believe me. If there had been another way, I would have found it. I allowed myself to get blindsided by the political machines in this city. I foolishly thought I was in control of what was going on, but it turned out I was only a pawn. As you have probably figured out, I'm used to being the one in charge. You can certainly imagine that admitting I was duped, to myself or to anyone else, is a bitter pill for me to swallow. "

I walked a little closer to him so I could see his face. "I'd like to understand. If you're willing to tell me, I'd like to hear what happened."

His face seemed to reflect a mixture of surprise and relief. "I'd like to tell you about all of it. But now isn't the time. Would you be willing to have dinner with me next week? I have to leave for D.C. tomorrow, but I'll be back at the end of the week. Why don't I plan to pick you up on Saturday at 7 pm? Hopefully, things will have settled down enough by then for me to be able to return to Nashville without worrying about a lynch mob. Although, that might be preferable to what I have to face with our board of directors."

He turned away from me and seemed to sink into deep thought. Again, my inclination was to reach out to him, to offer him some comfort from the misery that seemed to envelop him. Instead, I just agreed to our dinner plans and arranged for him to call me earlier that day to get directions to my apartment.

The night air had turned chilly, and I shivered as we walked to the valet stand. I realized I'd left my shawl somewhere, but I didn't want to return to the crowd to look for it. Jon must have noticed my shivering because he took off his suit coat and draped it across my shoulders. He pulled it snugly over my shoulders, allowing his right arm to remain around me. I was enjoying the warmth of our bodies pressed together and looked up with regret when I saw the valet pull my little Bug to the curb. Jon removed his jacket from my shoulders then helped me into the car. Before he closed the door, he leaned in and gently kissed my forehead. "Good night, Georgia. Please drive safely."

I could see him still standing on the curb as I drove away, and I kept glancing into my rearview mirror for a glimpse of him until he disappeared from sight. Ebie rushed at me with excitement when I unlocked the door to my apartment. I scooped her up in one arm as I went into the bedroom, dropping her gently on the comforter while being careful to avoid her front claws that were attempting to grab hold of my skirt.

I took off my gown and hung it carefully in the closet then replaced my undergarments with soft cotton pajamas. After washing the makeup off my face, I pulled on my robe and plopped on the bed beside her. "What a night I've had." She began to butt her head against my chest, so I lay back on the bed and allowed her to work her way up to where she snuggled against my neck.

That's the way it is with cats; they are unabashedly open about their feelings. When they're happy they let you know it with purrs and caresses. When they are displeased, it is clearly expressed by their looks of disapproval and audible expressions of dismay.

If only people were that easy to understand, I thought. The evening had taken more of a toll on me than I realized, and I could feel my eyes begin to grow heavy. My last thought before sleep claimed me was the question Jon asked me on the terrace: "Are you worth the risk?" After the mayor's announcement, and my shock at learning of Jon's role in the whole plan, I wasn't sure I was willing to risk *anything* in order to be around him again. I felt an undeniable pull toward him, but I couldn't decide if it was a pull I should give into, or one I should run from. I sighed deeply as I allowed sleep to pull the thoughts from my mind, only to reappear later in the form of unsettled dreams.

Chapter 15

Monday began one of the longest weeks of my life. I was still mentally wrestling with Jon's question, and trying to comprehend his announcement. The atmosphere around the building housing the two newspaper staffs was tense, as those of us on *The Nashville News* attempted to gingerly tread our way past our fellow reporters on *The Daily Courier*. No one said very much about what we heard at the dinner, at least not openly. But there was an undercurrent of anxiety and expectation that could be felt as clearly as the electricity that filled the air on a stormy day. Even the usually hectic and noisy newsroom was more reminiscent of a wake, without the array of alcohol to help the bereaved derive some semblance of cheer.

Only Mr. Stein appeared to have received the news in a way that gave levity to his usually ill-tempered mood. His door remained open through the day, and he emerged from it regularly to move through our ranks like a general surveying his troops. But, uncharacteristically, instead of issuing orders and questioning the work being performed, he doled out pats on the back and words of encouragement, leaving his recipients to stand frozen in shocked silence. Clearly, the news of *The Daily Courier's* impending demise was the fodder that fueled his transformation. I found myself wondering if he had been pre-advised of what was to occur. That would certainly explain why he made such an abrupt reversal of his directive that I pursue the good will of Jon Barnett. Perhaps he had been afraid that if I caught wind of the plan, I would somehow interfere with its accomplishment. I found the thought that I could have any impact at all on the outcome to be both flattering and ludicrous.

I tried to keep busy the rest of the week, which wasn't too difficult. Writing assignments continued to flow steadily in my direction, but by Friday I was beginning to feel the toll of trying to not think about what I really needed to think about. I decided a girls' night in with Julie was exactly what I needed.

We arranged to meet after work at my apartment. Julie arrived carrying two shopping bags which she began to unload on my kitchen counter.

"A six-pack each of Coke and beer, depending upon whether you feel the need to be stirred up or calmed down, chips and dip, and deli sandwiches from *Zager's.*" Her smile displayed smug satisfaction in a job well done.

"Perfect!" I said as I surveyed the spread. "I think I'll start with one of those beers."

She handed one to me and took one for herself. I suggested we take our drinks out onto the balcony, leading the way there as I snagged the bag of chips. The early evening air was wonderfully mild. We pulled the two chairs I kept on the balcony close to the railing so we could rest our feet while we surveyed the street below. Ebie came out to join us and stretched luxuriously in a patch of lingering sunlight on the balcony floor, rolling to scratch her back on the concrete before settling down for a snooze.

For a while, we sat in silence, sipping cold beer and munching chips. One of the things I valued about my friendship with Julie was that she was as comfortable with not speaking as she was with an animated conversation. Sometimes it even seemed we communicated more in the spaces between our words than we did through what was being said. Not that we didn't talk a lot to each other. Julie was good about bantering thoughts back and forth with me on pretty much any topic. She was just more inclined to hang back and listen, instead of rattling off every thought that popped into her head. In that respect, we were a good match. There were times when I really wanted to talk things through in minute detail, and others when I just wanted someone to keep me company while I mulled something over in my mind.

On this occasion, I was torn somewhere between the two. I wanted to talk about what was bothering me, but I first needed to figure it out somewhat before I was willing to risk saying it out loud. I found it difficult to separate my feelings about Jon's involvement in closing *The Daily Courier* from what I perceived as a growing personal connection between the two of us. Whenever I entertained fantasies about what sort of relationship I hoped to eventually have with a husband, it always involved deep trust and openness. With Jon, neither of those factors had been present since the day we first met. So, how could I possibly consider seeing him again in any capacity, other than a strictly professional one?

I knew the answer. I couldn't see him again, at least not alone, unless I intended to open the door to any possibility that might develop between us. But why would I want to do that? Hadn't he proven to be unreliable, and certainly unpredictable, enough times to warn me off?

I felt a nudge on my foot as Julie reached over to tap me with her shoe. "Are you going to let me in on it, or do you intend to sit out here and stew in your own misery?"

I sighed and took a deep swallow of my beer. "Why does life have to be so complicated? Don't you sometimes just wish you could go back to the sweet oblivion of childhood?"

She shook her head emphatically. "No way. My childhood was certainly no piece of cake. I'd take the struggles of being an adult over those years any time."

I nodded my head in understanding. Although our childhoods had been as different as they could possibly be, we had each been the recipient of more than our share of trials and tribulations. Julie grew up in a family of five children who, as she described it, were always competing with one another for everything. As a result, her life at home was raucous at best, nerve rattling at its worst. Since Julie's position on the sibling roster was that of the third born of the five, she frequently fell into the role of peacemaker, often intervening in the battles generated by her siblings while her parents were otherwise occupied. In essence, she had received years of "on the job" training in the fine art of conflict resolution, which also gave her the unique ability of knowing when to stay silent, and when to speak up.

I, on the other hand, was the only child of parents who had never failed to let me know I was a mistake of nature. My childhood years were spent trying to make myself as invisible as possible, in an effort to avoid drawing attention to my existence. As a result, I was forced to pass countless hours alone, many of which were spent lost in fantasies of my own creation. I liked to think this had given me the active imagination that contributed to my writing prowess. But I think it really only made me a loner. Until I met Julie, I never developed a sense of comfort with expressing my feelings out loud to anyone else, choosing instead the safety of hashing them over in my own mind. Julie had been the first person who made me feel safe putting my feelings into words. The solace I felt as a child spending time with my Nanna was not because of anything she said to me. We never talked about my feelings of being unwanted by my parents. Nonetheless, I always felt certain of her love for me. That was the first time I understood that feelings did not have to be put into words in order to be real. It was often the things left unsaid that carried the greatest weight, for better, and for worse. But it was a special gift to be able to voice my thoughts out loud to Julie without worrying about being rejected.

"You're right, of course. I guess I forgot for a minute how difficult it was to be a child, at least in *our* experiences."

Julie nodded her understanding then hopped from the chair and stretched her arms over her head. "I love Friday nights. It's so satisfying to know the whole weekend is waiting to be enjoyed in any way I choose." She picked up her now empty beer bottle. "I'm going to have another one and some of that dip I brought. You want one?"

I held my half-full bottle up to the light. "No thanks. I'd better stick to one, until I work things through in my head. I don't want alcohol clouding the picture."

"Hum. Seems to me a little clouding might be just what you need. It might help you let go of that tight rein you always keep on yourself." She walked toward the door. "I'll be right back. Hopefully, by then you'll be ready to tell me what's on your mind."

She returned a few minutes later and placed two small tray tables between us. She spread out plates, napkins, the chips, dip, and the sandwiches she brought, then loaded a plate with food before sitting. She turned to face me. "Now. What's going on?"

I placed my own beer on the nearby table and munched on a chip. "I told you what happened at the dinner; about the mayor's announcement, Jon's comments, and how he asked if he could take me out to dinner tomorrow night." She nodded. "What I didn't tell you is that Jon also said something to me before dinner about how he wondered if I was worth the risk. I've been trying to figure out what he meant."

She narrowed her eyes. "What was he talking about before he said that?"

I tried to recall the exact details of the conversation. "Something about how it's good to be unpredictable and to explore new things, even if it means we might be disappointed with what we find."

She took a hearty bite of her sandwich and chewed energetically before answering. "Sounds like he was saying he wants to get to know you better, but he wants you to reassure him you're interested in getting to know him. too. Somehow that doesn't sound like the cocky, self-assured man you've described before."

What she said was true. He hadn't seemed as confident that night as he had on previous occasions. Especially after the

Mayor made his announcement. When we talked outside afterward, he seemed sad and a little vulnerable, almost like he needed comforting. That was very different from the way he always acted.

I remembered what Miss Hood said about him. I wondered if there was something we shared that had been hidden away until now. Just as I had been molded into the person I am by my early experiences, maybe he was also a product of his family's expectations. I realized I had never thought of him as someone with a past that might not have been perfect. The thought made me feel a little less afraid. *Afraid?* Yes, that was it. I had been afraid to get to know him or, more precisely, to let him get to know me. My fear was that he would be disappointed if he knew who I really was, and he would push me away. Basically, I was afraid I would get hurt.

Maybe that's what I had been worried about all along; if I let him close, if I started to care what he felt for me, he would repeat the pattern I experienced throughout my childhood and tell me I was unworthy of his attention. I would experience the hurt of rejection all over again. It seems some of us choose to carry our past around like a backpack loaded with rocks. We trudge along bearing the weight as if it is molded to our backs, not realizing we can actually take it off. The load we carry forces us to slow down our forward progress. Even if we stop to remove a little of the weight, we still struggle to right ourselves and regain our balance. As a result, we're always a little off-kilter.

That's what I had been feeling ever since I met Jon; off-balance. His piercing looks and cryptic remarks threatened to throw off the equilibrium of my life. I was beginning to realize, regardless of how precarious that balance really was, it was familiar, and I was reluctant to give it up.

I set down my plate and looked at Julie. She had been sitting patiently while I held this internal monologue with myself. I sat up straighter in my chair to face her. "I think I know what I want to do. What I have to do. It's time for me to grow up and stop being afraid of everything. "

Julie's smile suggested she agreed with me. Once more my friend knew when to keep her counsel to herself. She lifted her bottle and gestured for me to do the same. "Here's to figuring out what we really want, and having the courage to pursue it when we do." We clinked bottles, then leaned back in our chairs to watch the last of the evening light fade into darkness.

Chapter 16

Regardless of my bravado of the night before, by Saturday evening, I felt like an over-tuned guitar string on the verge of snapping. Jon phoned earlier in the day to let me know he was back in town, and to confirm he would be by to pick me up at seven o'clock that evening. I spent a good two hours pulling clothes out of my closet, then dropping them on an ever-growing pile of rejects, finally settling on a plain pair of black dress slacks and a beige silk sweater. I planned to dress it up with some gold jewelry Nanna left me, and a black and gold printed scarf I found at *Harvey's* department store the previous winter. A pair of black patent-leather high heels would complete the ensemble. I was glad, even with two inches added to my height, Jon would tower over me by at least half a foot.

Even though I chose my outfit well in advance of seven o'clock, I still found myself rushing to get ready on time. I was just applying the last of my make-up, which only amounted to a little mascara and lipstick, when I heard a knock on the door. Ebie, who had been watching my flurry of activity from her favorite spot on my bed, looked up in anticipation. I opened the door to reveal

Jon standing in the hallway holding a bouquet of flowers and a small gray box wrapped with a large white bow.

He was wearing a pair of light gray dress slacks with an open-collared white shirt and a navy sport coat. He looked *delicious!*

"Georgia." His eyes seemed to scan my body from head to toe. "You look lovely. These are for you." He handed me the flowers and box.

"Thank you, Jon. I wasn't sure how to dress. I hope this is okay." I took the flowers into the kitchen to search for something appropriate to put them in, finally settling on a tall water glass.

"It's perfect. I should have told you where we were going so you wouldn't have to worry. I've made reservations at a place called *Ireland's,* not far from here. "

Ireland's was a locally run establishment famous for its steak and biscuits. A dimly lit back room provided a safe haven for discrete trysts, as well as secret meetings of the local music industry executives and the performers they were attempting to impress. I had been there a few times in the past, but not recently. The thought of sinking my teeth into one of their specialties had my mouth watering.

"That's one of my favorite places. They have incredible steak and biscuits." My hands were fidgeting with the ribbon on the box I placed on the kitchen counter while I put the flowers in the glass.

"Why don't you open that?" He gestured at the box.

I carefully untied the bow and opened the top. There was a pad of cotton inside that hid the contents from view. I removed it to reveal a gold filigree broach in the shape of a four-leaf clover.

"I saw that while I was in D.C. this week and thought of you. Your last name is Irish, isn't it?" He asked.

"Yes, on my father's side. It's so lovely!"

He reached into the box. "May I pin it on for you?"

I held my breath as he unclasped the pin and reached to attach it to my scarf. I could feel his warm breath on my face and

I could detect the faint scent of his aftershave, which reminded me of leather and cinnamon. He raised his head to look at the broach but remained standing close to me.

"There. It suits you."

I averted my eyes from his and reached down to finger the delicate weaving of the piece. "It was so nice of you to think of me. It's beautiful."

He reached out to lift my chin up with one finger. "You're beautiful. I'm afraid it pales by comparison." He looked deeply into my eyes.

I could feel my heart thumping and all I could think about was getting away from his gaze. I turned to the side and began to collect the contents of the empty box, hoping that my discomfort was not apparent. Luckily, he took a step back, as well, and I let out a silent breath.

His eyes took in the contents of my apartment, settling on Ebie who was watching us curiously from the kitchen doorway. "Hello, little one. What's your name?"

He crouched down to gaze at Ebie who, to my surprise, marched right up to him with a coquettish look. He reached out a hand and caressed her head. "Aren't you a pretty girl?" Ebie began to purr and rub her head against his hand. Apparently, Jon's talent for impressing the ladies also extended to the feline type. "What's her name?" he asked.

"Ebie. Short for Ebony. So, you like cats?"

He stood but kept looking down at her. "I always wanted one when I was growing up, but my parents were against having pets. They said pets were a distraction from our schoolwork, although I always suspected they just didn't want them messing up their orderly house. My sister and I used to fight over whether we'd get a dog or a cat, even though we knew deep down we weren't likely to have either. Jen was more of a dog person than me. I guess we were the opposite of most people in that respect. I've always had a soft spot for cats."

"I didn't know you have a sister." There it was again; his ever-present knack for surprising me.

His face lit up with a smile of pure joy. "Jen's six years younger than me. My parents were trying for the perfect match of one boy and one girl for several years before Jen came along. I never really got the impression that being parents mattered very much to them. It was more of a status thing." His smile faded into a solemn expression as he spoke. "When Jen was born, I fell totally in love with her. Once she was old enough to walk, she used to tag along after me everywhere I went. When I became a teenager, I found her adoration aggravating, and I tried to ignore her so she would leave me alone. Apparently, it worked because we had very little to do with each other for several years. It was only when we both became adults that we grew close again."

"Where is she now?" I asked.

"She's living just outside of D.C., in Arlington, Virginia, with her husband and three sons. They're a great family. I try to stop by to see them whenever I'm up that way. In fact, I had dinner with them last week."

My mind was trying to absorb these newly discovered images of Jon *the pet lover*, *the big brother*, and *the uncle*. My heart softened at seeing the way he responded to Ebie. It was turning into a pile of warm mush as I imagined him looking out for his little sister, or tossing around a ball with his nephews. Yes, this man was definitely not who he appeared to be on the surface. Realizing that helped ease my own discomfort at being around him. He began to seem more real to me, in some respects. He was just a human being like the rest of us, with private feelings and apparently even some secret hurts. But he also seemed to feel the need to keep them hidden away behind a hard facade. He had cracked open its surface a little bit tonight, and I hoped he would continue to allow me to see what was inside.

He glanced at his watch and suggested we leave for the restaurant. I was feeling a little reluctant to break the spell of closeness that had come over us, but I followed him out the door and down the stairs to the curb where a sleek, black sports car was parked. "Is this yours?" I asked.

He nodded. "I leased it last week. I got tired of riding in taxis everywhere. Since I'm unsure how long I'll be staying around, I thought leasing made more sense than buying." He opened the door to the passenger side and offered me a hand. I ducked my head and slid onto the leather seat. I was surprised at how luxuriously soft it felt, and I caressed the smooth leather as I waited for him to slide into the driver's seat. I also noticed the inside of his car held the same scent I smelled on him earlier in the evening. I realized it must have come from the mingled aroma of new leather and some sort of spicy aftershave.

We rode in silence to the restaurant, just a short drive from my apartment. The hostess led us to a booth in the back room that was quieter and more subtly lit than the rest of the dining area. The restaurant was not especially crowded for a Saturday night, but there were a few larger parties raising the volume of the entire place with their laughter and loud conversation. To my surprise, Jon waited for me to take a seat on one side of the booth then scooted in next to me.

"I hope you don't mind. I thought it would be easier to hear each other if I sat next to you."

"No, it's fine." I ducked my head to hide my pleasure and began to scan the menu. Jon placed a drink order with the waitress, who returned shortly with a scotch on the rocks for Jon and a gin and tonic for me. I wasn't sure if I would be able to force down any drink that contained gin, but since it wasn't matched with *Kool-Aid*, I decided to give it a try. When the drinks were placed in front of us, Jon asked for two orders of steak and biscuits then turned slightly to angle his body in my direction.

"Here's to you." He lifted his glass and touched it to mine. I took a tentative sip and was surprised to find the taste was pleasant. He took a hearty swallow of his drink then placed it on the table, moving his right hand to cover my left. "Tell me what you've been doing since I last saw you. I realized, while I was away, the only thing I really know about you is that you're a reporter. I want to know how you spend your time when you're not attending Grand Balls or insulting unsuspecting male admirers."

His comment brought back the memory of the night we first met. It felt like such a long time ago. I was surprised to realize it had only been a couple of months. "That was an odd evening. It was actually my first real reporting assignment, and I was more than a little uncomfortable."

His eyebrows lifted as he considered what I said. "I wasn't aware of that, but now that you mention it, you did seem a little out of your element."

While what he said was true, I found myself bristling at the implication that I didn't look like I quite fit in with the guests at the Ball. *Was he trying to insult me, or was this just another example of his tendency to keep me off-balance?* I could feel myself closing off to him emotionally, and I shifted on the bench so I could put more physical distance between us. "Sometimes I don't know what to make of the things you say."

His head lifted, as if my comment surprised him, then he nodded in agreement. "I apologize. I'm afraid that's a Barnett family trait. Always keep the other party guessing. We like to think it gives us the upper hand in negotiations."

"Does it always work? Something you said at Mr. Stein's dinner gave me the impression you felt things went very wrong when it came to your efforts to negotiate the purchase of *The Daily Courier*."

He frowned. "That was a good example of what can happen when you let people in on what you're thinking. I made the mistake of trusting the Mayor with my family's plans to buy *The Daily Courier* and relocate its production to the Belmont Mansion. We intended to make it a part of the journalism program there, and involve the students in the entire process of putting out a newspaper. What I didn't realize, until it was too late, was the mayor had more to gain by shutting the paper down. So, he effectively blocked our acquisition of the Mansion. But not before he helped smooth the way for the purchase of the newspaper. We were locked into the deal before I knew what happened. That's why I was so angry that day I came by the MHC office. I convinced myself that Ida Hood knew what I had in mind, and she was instrumental in the entire scheme. I realized later; she was just as much of an innocent party as I." He paused while the waitress placed our meals in front of us and signaled her to bring him a fresh drink. "I want you to know it was my intention from the beginning to buy the paper in order to give it new life in a slightly different venue. I was as distressed as anyone at the way things turned out."

"Are you sure there isn't another way to save the paper? What about finding another place to relocate?"

He shook his head. "That's why I went to D.C. this week; to see if our board members could use their collective heads to come up with a solution. But we're running out of time. The deadline for finalizing the sale is next week. *The Daily Courier* will end publication on the first of May. That means we would have to really hustle to find an alternate site for its relocation in just a little over two months. That's a lot less time than we had to work on our original plan. Since we'd banked all our hopes on using the Mansion, we didn't seriously consider any other options. As I said at the dinner, we were duped. Or, to put it more accurately, I was."

A plan had begun to form in my mind as he spoke. "I may have an idea, but I need to check something out first."

He shook his head solemnly. "Believe me, if there was a way around this, we would have found it. I appreciate you wanting to help, but it's better to just let this one go."

I placed a hand carefully on his arm and smiled in what I hoped was a reassuring way. "Just give me a day to look into something. If I have nothing to offer at that point, I promise I'll drop the subject."

His eyes still looked grave. "I don't know what you have in mind, but I'm willing to wait a day to find out. Now, let's make a pact to stop talking about work for the rest of the evening, and just enjoy ourselves." He glanced at his plate. "These steak and biscuits look great. I just realized how hungry I am." He picked one up and took a generous bite. "Umm. Now I know why they're famous for these little gems. They're incredible." He finished off the first biscuit and reached for a second.

I looked down at my plate, but my mind was so full of ideas, I found it difficult to focus on the food in front of me, or the man next to me. If what I had in mind worked, it would pull off the biggest coup ever. I could hardly wait for the morning to come so I could set my plan in motion.

Chapter 17

The rest of the evening went well. Jon shared stories with me about his childhood and I tentatively described a little of mine. By the time the evening ended, we were both more relaxed and even managed to laugh quite a bit. We parted company after Jon walked me to the door and gave me a gentle kiss. It wasn't exactly what I had expected. Actually, I'm not sure what I expected, but I found myself a little disappointed that his goodnight kiss seemed so empty of passion. I decided to chalk it up to his fatigue, rather than follow my usual tendency to interpret it as some shortcoming of my own.

By midday Sunday, I worked out more of the details of the plan I had in mind, but I needed one crucial addition before I could set it in motion; Ida Hood. Something she said at one of our meetings stuck in my head, and I needed to talk to her about it. She had given me her address and phone number after I wrote the story about her aunt, so I decided to ring her to see if I could stop by her house. To my relief, she welcomed my visit, and even suggested I come by later that afternoon.

Her house was located in the neighborhood to the west of Belmont College. It was a two-story brick home with a small front yard bordered by neatly trimmed flower gardens. I parked on the street in front, and made my way up the potted plant lined walkway leading to her door. I took a deep breath before ringing her doorbell. My excitement over the idea brewing in my mind since the previous night had me vibrating like an overload of caffeine. She opened the door promptly and ushered me into a front hallway with doors that opened into rooms on either side. I followed her into the room on the right, which turned out to be a comfortable sitting area containing an overstuffed couch, flanked on each end by tables holding lamps that appeared to be antiques. Two wingback chairs were placed adjacent to the tables, and the entire arrangement made a cozy semi-circle around a fireplace that glowed with the welcoming warmth of a wood fire. The room was filled with the delicious scent of pine and something else that hinted of herbs. A medium-sized, marble-topped wooden cocktail table sat in front of the couch holding a tray covered with small sandwiches and a pot of something hot, which seemed to be the source of the herb scent. The entire room felt like being enveloped in a big, warm hug, and I smiled with affection for the woman who arranged such a welcoming place.

"Oh, Miss Hood, this is wonderful. I would never be able to leave this room if I lived here."

She smiled with obvious delight. "Please, hang your coat on that rack behind you and take a seat. I'm so glad you called. Sundays can feel a bit long at times. I'm excited to have your company, and by the way, I think it's time you called me by my first name. I appreciate your show of respect for our obvious age difference, but I feel like we've become well enough acquainted by now that we should be on a first name basis."

Her sentiment touched me deeply, and I ducked my head in an attempt to hide the blush I knew must be covering my face. "If you're sure that's alright, I would be honored." I sat on one end of the couch while she chose the chair closest to me.

She leaned forward and lifted the pot. "Would you care for some tea? I thought it would be a nice change from coffee.

There are also some pimento cheese and ham sandwiches in case you're hungry."

My stomach rumbled in anticipation of the treats. I realized I hadn't eaten anything since my morning coffee and half of an English muffin. Although my appetite was never what one would call "large", at least not by most standards, forgetting to eat was something that rarely happened to me. It suggested I had been more than a little preoccupied with my deliberations. "It looks delicious, but I didn't want you to go to any trouble. I'm just grateful you agreed to see me today."

She waved her hand to indicate it was no bother. I placed one of each of the sandwiches on my plate and lifted the cup she poured for me. It gave off a faint aroma of oranges and something else that I couldn't identify.

"I hope you like the tea. It's *Constant Comment* with a few sprigs of mint from my backyard. I find it gives the tea a bit of pizazz."

I took a sip and nodded my agreement. "It's good. I would never have thought to add mint, but it's very refreshing."

She smiled with pleasure and lifted her own cup, settling back comfortably into her chair. "Now. Tell me what this is all about. You seemed quite anxious to talk to me about something."

I placed my cup on the table. "I suppose you've heard about what happened with *The Daily Courier*? How the Barnett family is going to purchase it then close it down?"

"Yes. I read about that in the paper. Unfortunate news, I think, except perhaps for the Mayor."

I looked at her in surprise. The article didn't say anything directly about Mayor Brill's involvement. I wondered how she could have figured out the political undertones of the decision.

"Don't look so shocked. It's no secret in this town that Mayor Brill has a lot to gain from silencing *The Daily Courier*. Its reports of his political activities have been far from favorable since before he was first elected. Word has it, their criticism almost cost him the re-election. No, I wouldn't think Bradford Brill would lose any sleep at all over *The Daily Courier's* demise."

She took a sip of her tea and regarded me closely. "What does Jon Barnett think about the decision?"

I finished the last bite of my first sandwich and reached for the second. "Actually, he's very upset. He claims it was never his intention to close *The Daily Courier*. He wanted to buy it and move the production to the Belmont mansion so it could become part of an expanded Journalism program at the school. A sort of training ground for the students, as he explained it."

Ida nodded slowly. "I see. So that's what he had in mind. I wish he had explained that upfront. I might have been able to help."

I put down my now empty plate and folded my hands in my lap. "Actually, that's what I wanted to talk to you about. I think there's a way you still might be able to help. You mentioned to me one time that your aunt left you some money you had hoped to use to help restore the mansion. Now that it has been designated as a historical treasure, those funds will be provided by the state." I took another sip of my tea. "I wonder if you would be willing to consider using some of your inheritance to add a wing onto the Mansion to serve as the new home for *The Daily Courier*. It could be done in a way that is consistent with the historical design of the building. By using it to expand Belmont's journalism program, you'd be carrying on the work of your aunt."

She leaned forward and rested her face on her hands. "That's an interesting idea. So, you're suggesting *The Daily Courier* would become a college-run newspaper, at least in principle. Of course, some of the current staff would have to stay on in order to provide instruction and guidance to the students." She tapped her fingers on her chin as she mulled over the idea. "Do you think they'd be willing to do that? It would require a significant change in their daily operations."

As she spoke, I began to see the plan I proposed was a lot more complex than I had considered. If it were to be realized, it would take more than just a physical relocation of the facilities. The staff would have to be trained in the proper methods of working with students, which meant actual educators would need to be hired to provide the training. It also meant the administrators of Belmont College would not only have to agree with the concept, but be willing to embrace it wholeheartedly. I began to feel discouraged about how much work would need to be done before any of this could materialize. As Jon had pointed out, the sale of *The Daily Courier* was to be finalized sometime during the next week.

I felt my earlier excitement begin to fade as the magnitude of the undertaking started to sink in. "Maybe this wasn't such a great idea. I'm afraid I didn't think things through as thoroughly as I should have."

Ida stood and began walking towards the entrance hall. For a moment, I thought she intended to show me out, then I noticed she was reaching for a telephone on the hall table. "Just let me make a call. I believe the Journalism program is housed in the Communications department. The head of that department is the son of an old friend of mine. I've known him since he was just a little boy, and I've always found him to be very open to interesting ideas. I'll just run this by him to see what he thinks."

I stood and followed her into the hall. "Does that mean you'd be willing to put up the money for the new wing? That is, if your friend thinks it's a good idea."

Her eyes danced with excitement as she turned to look at me. "You've certainly given me something to think about. Let's just see what he has to say before we take this any further. We don't want to put the cart in front of the horse." She reached into a drawer on the hall table and pulled out an envelope. "Here. Why don't you read this while you're waiting? It may help you understand why this just may work."

The envelope contained a letter addressed to her and signed by a Thomas Bookman. It began in the same way as most letters between friends, then launched into a description of how Mr. Bookman left his job in upstate New York to come to Nashville to help establish a Journalism program at Belmont College. The letter contained a clipping from the paper he had worked for in New York explaining his involvement in pioneering the use of *New Journalism*, which he described involved a style of writing most often associated with works of fiction for reporting news events. From what I could understand, it was intended to provide the reader with an interesting story to read, much like that of a well-versed novel, but with the twist that everything they were reading actually happened. It was essentially non-fiction that reads like fiction.

As I continued perusing the letter, I found it interesting to discover that Thomas Bookman had initially worked as a part-time news reporter for *The Daily Courier* during the same time he held a faculty position at Belmont College. He left *The Daily Courier* due to continuous disagreements with the editors who viewed his writing style as too unconventional for their tastes. In his concluding comments, he expressed his dismay that his belief in the value of *New Journalism* was not shared by either of the local newspapers in Nashville, and how he hoped, over time, this would change.

As I finished the letter, I heard Ida say, "Oh, that's wonderful, Thomas! We'll be sure to do that." She hung up the phone and turned to me with a satisfied grin. "He said he'd be delighted to talk to us about your idea.

He suggested we call his secretary first thing tomorrow morning to set up an appointment."

I handed the letter to her. "Do you think he'd be willing to support relocating *The Daily Courier* to the college, given the struggles he's had with the editors? This letter suggests he may not be so keen on forming a lasting association with either of our local papers."

She returned the letter to the table drawer. "He didn't go so far as to say he would. He's too good of a journalist to commit to something without thoroughly researching it. But I could detect a fairly high level of excitement in his voice. I think it would be fair to say that if there were no unforeseen problems, Thomas would jump at the chance to take over the reins of *The Daily Courier*. It just might be the ticket out of the quandary he's in."

"I guess you're referring to his interest in convincing the paper to use this *New Journalism* style of writing he talked about in his letter. I have to admit, I've never heard anything about it." She nodded. "I'm not surprised. It's still considered very avant-garde in most journalism circles. Only the most adventurous papers have embraced the style, and that certainly doesn't describe what we know of *The Daily Courier*, or *The Nashville News*, for that matter."

An idea began to form in my mind. If we were successful at pulling off this move, it would not only save *The Daily Courier* from closure, but it could also be the driving force behind a renovation in news reporting, as I knew it. I wasn't sure how comfortable I felt about that, since it wasn't something I had any experience with. But the idea of being on the forefront of something that could change the face of journalism in Nashville, and certainly alter the career I had chosen for myself, was incredibly exciting, and scary! Exactly what it would mean for my future on *The Nashville News,* I couldn't predict. It was quite possible the higher-ups on *The Nashville News* would look upon this new style of writing with as much scorn as their cohorts did on *The Daily Courier*. That I could be instrumental in pulling off a move that would not only continue the chief source of their competition, but also help develop a program which would turn out a whole slew of fledgling reporters trained in *New Journalism*, might end up bringing me more trouble than I was prepared to deal with.

Ida and I agreed she would be the one to call to set up the appointment with Thomas Bookman, then phone to let me know when the meeting would take place. The last thing she said to me as I left her house, was to encourage me to have faith that things would work out the way they were meant to, because "life is either a daring adventure or nothing at all". I wasn't sure if that idea comforted me, or just added to my fear. It was clear I had been a party to more adventures during the past few weeks than I could remember encountering during the entirety of my life. It didn't look like things were about to change anytime soon.

Chapter 18

The meeting with Thomas Bookman was set for the next afternoon, which was great considering the time crunch we were under to set things in motion. We were instructed to go to his office on the Belmont campus at 6 P.M., which was late enough to allow me to slip away from work without drawing any attention to my absence. My usual workday started by 9 A.M. and ended around 5:30 or 6 P.M., though there had been times when I was still on assignment until late in the evening.

I picked up Ida on the way to Belmont so we could arrive at the meeting together. The Communications Department, which included the Journalism program, was housed in a gray stone building adjacent to the Mansion. There were a few students lingering outside the building when we arrived, and one of them directed us to Mr. Bookman's office. The door to his office was wide open. We tapped on the frame and a sandy haired man poked his head around the corner of a bookcase. "Ida? Come in, come in!"

He wove his way around a desk stacked high with newspapers and books, then lifted a pile of what looked like test papers off a chair in front of the desk. "Let me just move this out of the way." His face was lit by a huge grin and his eyes sparkled brightly behind a pair of rimless glasses. I expected a much older man, given the list of accomplishments Ida had credited him with. I was surprised to find he appeared to be only in his early thirties. He dropped the papers onto the floor to the left of the door and reached to embrace Ida warmly. "How have you been? My father said to tell you you've kept yourself locked up down here for far too long."

Ida's face showed her pleasure as she returned his hug then pulled back to study him. "You look like him, you know. Or at least, you look like the young man I knew many years ago. How is he?"

Thomas smiled and shook his head. "As ornery as ever. Since his retirement, he's been giving my mother fits trying to keep him occupied. Says retiring was the worst mistake he's ever made, and I think she tends to agree with him. Of course, they didn't give him much choice. After his heart attack, the bureau told him he'd either have to retire or take a desk job, and you can imagine how well that would have gone over."

Ida explained that Thomas' father had been a police officer in Brooklyn, New York for a little over thirty years prior to his retirement. He finished his tenure at the rank of Captain. I guessed his father must be a couple of decades younger than Ida.

"I went to New York to try to locate my niece, Beth. She moved to New York after graduating from Ward-Belmont then disappeared from sight. Luckily, it turned out she hadn't really disappeared so much as chosen to hide. Apparently, she met and moved in with a young man shortly after arriving in New York. Since she knew her parents wouldn't approve of her arrangement, she chose to avoid facing them with the truth. It was all very unfortunate, but at least, she hadn't come to any harm."

Thomas put his hand affectionately on Ida's shoulder. "Ida showed up in New York determined to find the girl. She ended up in my dad's precinct demanding someone do something to locate her. Luckily, my dad wandered by at the exact moment she looked ready to take on the officer on duty, and pulled her off into his office for a cup of coffee. Since it was the end of his shift, he brought her home for dinner after convincing her it was the safest thing for her to do, given that she had arrived in the city without any plans about where to stay. She and my mom hit it off right away, and that was the start of a lifelong friendship between the three of them."

Ida smiled up at him warmly. "Your parents were so kind to take me in. I'm afraid I was a little hot-headed in those days."

Thomas laughed. "No more so than my dad. I'm surprised the two of you became friends, given how similar you are in that respect."

Ida shrugged and looked at me. "Sometimes there's no explanation for why two people become friends. It's not something you can plan, and it usually doesn't work out if you try to force it. But if there's one thing I've learned in my life, it's to embrace the gift of friendship, however it comes along. Sometimes that gift shows up when you least expect it, like the day Georgia found her way to my office." She smiled at me warmly.

Her words touched me. I hadn't really thought about it until now, but it was true that Ida and I had become friends, despite the fifty years separating us in age and a world of difference in what we had experienced in our lives. But I guessed she was right. Friendship is a gift you shouldn't question, whenever, wherever, and in whatever form it appears.

Over the next hour, Thomas described his past and present experiences in trying to spearhead a movement to embrace the new journalistic style he had alluded to in his letter. His passion about *New Journalism* was clearly evident, and I couldn't help but become caught up in his enthusiasm. I was, however, more than a little disappointed to find out that the Journalism program at Belmont was very sparsely populated, consisting of only one full-time faculty member...Thomas, who actually spread his time between that program and his duties as chair of the Communications Department. The rest of the Journalism program staff consisted of two part-time faculty members, and one secretary, who was shared among the three. When Ida described him as the head of the department, I imagined a slew of faculty and staff members, all of whom reported to him. The truth fell far short of my imagination. I wondered what impact that would have on our ability to set in motion the plan that we had in mind.

Ida and Thomas didn't seem to share my concerns. By the time our meeting ended, they had mapped out the next steps in a strategy intended to launch the relocation of *The Daily Courier*. Unfortunately, what was left to do in order to set that plan in motion was no small undertaking. Nonetheless, I found myself excited by the prospects. By the time we left his office, I was feeling surprisingly optimistic about the potential of actually seeing our ideas take form.

I dropped Ida off at her home, and we agreed to get in touch with each other the following day to discuss our next steps. The job assigned to me was to talk to Jon about our idea in order to make sure he and his family wouldn't oppose it. I honestly had no idea how he would react to what I had to tell him, and I was a little nervous about bringing it up. But the plan was not far off from what he originally intended to do with *The Daily Courier*. I had high hopes his response would be positive.

I didn't have to wait long to find out. When I arrived home that evening, I spotted Jon's car parked on the street in front of my apartment. I pulled into a parking space on the curb behind him and walked forward to peer into the car windows. The car was empty. I looked up and down the street to see if I could spot him. I turned toward my apartment building, and noticed a figure sitting on the steps. The night had grown dark, with only a small bulb hanging over the entrance door to light the steps. The thudding of my heart told me the person sitting there was Jon.

I walked toward him, and he stood up stiffly. "These steps obviously weren't made for comfort." He placed his hands on his hips and arched his back.

"No, I suppose they're not. I'm surprised to see you here. Did we have plans to meet tonight?" I moved close enough to see his face, which appeared tired and unshaven.

"No, but I've been expecting to hear from you after what you said at the end of our dinner the other night. You really should get an answering machine, you know. I must have phoned you a dozen times."

I had heard the same admonishment from more than one person. I wasn't sure why I was reluctant to purchase one of the new machines, except I essentially liked the idea of being unavailable at times.

"I'm sorry. I've been planning to call you, but I've been waiting until I had something worthwhile to say. I've just come from a meeting where I heard some exciting news. I was planning to phone you this evening. Why don't you come inside where we can talk more comfortably?"

"If that plan includes a stiff drink and something to eat, you're on." I smiled at his grimace as he rolled his shoulders and attempted to straighten his back.

"I think I can manage that. Just let me grab my things from the car."

A few minutes later we were inside my apartment where Ebie with dancing around our legs. Jon sat slumped on the sofa, and Ebie quickly claimed a spot on his lap. I went into the bedroom to put down my work satchel and purse and quickly checked my appearance in the dresser mirror. I gave a few quick brush strokes to my hair, deciding there was little else I could do to improve things at that point, then went to check out the contents of my refrigerator.

I don't know what I was expecting to find in there, since it rarely contained anything more than leftover take-out containers, or the rudimentary makings for a sandwich. I kept telling myself I should stock up on some real food one of these days, but I never seemed to get around to it. I turned from the open door and gave Jon an apologetic look. "I'm afraid I don't have anything stronger to drink than beer, but there's some leftover chicken and potato salad we could have for dinner."

He shook his head and groaned slightly. "Beer will be fine. Let's start with that."

I took two bottles from the refrigerator and handed one to Jon. "Would you like a glass for that?"

"Bottle's good." He patted the cushion next to him. "Sit and tell me about your exciting meeting."

I joined Jon on the sofa and described the events of the past couple of days that led to my meeting Thomas Bookman. I tried to explain things as accurately as possible, without injecting too much of my possibly misguided optimism, so he would have a chance to form his own opinion. Jon listened quietly as I spoke, which gave me no clue as to how he was reacting to my news. When I finished, he placed his half-finished beer on the floor and turned to look at me. His face seemed to have relaxed some from when I first saw him sitting on my doorstep, but I wasn't sure if that was from the beer or the story I shared with him.

He shook his head from side to side as his face broke into a grin. "That's an amazing story. YOU are an amazing woman. How did you even come up with an idea like that?"

I squirmed a little under the intensity of his gaze and the surprising flattery. "It was as much Ida's idea as mine. She's the one who thought of Thomas Bookman. If it wasn't for her contacts and her money, none of this would be even remotely possible." I looked at him curiously. "Are you saying you think it's a good idea?"

He picked up his beer and took another sip. "I'm not saying it is or it isn't. But I do think it's worth a shot. I'm somewhat familiar with this New Journalism you mentioned. It has some pretty staunch followers in certain circles within the newspaper business, but it also has a great deal of opposition too. My family and I have never shied away from controversy, as you have most likely figured out by now. But, as you can imagine, I think the idea of relocating offices of *The Daily Courier* to Belmont has a lot of merit. I thought that possibility was off the table, but you may have just figured out a way to make it happen." He reached over and took my hand in his. "Thank you, Georgia. You have no idea what your efforts mean to me."

I noticed my hand fit neatly into his, and I could feel the warmth of his touch all the way into the center of my chest. "I'm glad you feel that way. I was nervous to talk to you about this." He looked at me with surprise. "Why? Did you think I wouldn't approve?" I shrugged. "I guess. Despite what you said, I wasn't really sure what you had in mind for *The Daily Courier*. You said you didn't want it to be shut down, but I wasn't sure you really meant it."

He sighed and looked at our joined hands. "I suppose I haven't given you a lot of reason to trust me, have I? I'm afraid my business dealings often require me to adopt a certain air of stern aloofness. Unfortunately, I tend to let that impression carry over to my personal relationships, too." His thumb rubbed the top of my hand as he stared off into space. "I'd like to try to remedy that, if you'll let me." He squeezed my hand gently before releasing it. "Let's start with me being honest with you about something."

I released the breath I hadn't realized I had been holding and sat up straighter on the sofa. My mind began to turn over the possibilities of what he might say. "What is it?" I asked.

He smiled. "I really don't care for beer. I like fried chicken and potato salad even less. If we're going to spend time with each other, you're going to have to do something about the contents of your refrigerator."

I laughed out loud. "Is that what you wanted to say? I thought it was going to be something really serious."

His eyes glinted with humor. "I happen to think food and drink are very serious subjects. Especially when I'm starving, which I happen to be. Are you sure you don't have anything else around here worth eating?"

I hopped up from the sofa and strode over to the refrigerator so I could examine its contents in more detail. "Some eggs, peanut butter, bread, and cheese. I'm afraid that's about it."

He clapped his hands and stood up. "Great! How does a cheese omelet and peanut butter toast sound?"

119

I looked at him doubtfully. "Like something I wish I knew how to make."

"Then you're in luck. That was one of my favorite meals in college. It was cheap, easy, and good any time of the day or night." He rubbed his hands together. "Just point me in the direction of a skillet then sit back and watch the master at work."

I had heard it said before, by a few of my more experienced female acquaintances, but there was something surprisingly sexy about watching a man cook. Maybe it was the uniqueness of the image, since most men I had been around seemed to regard the kitchen as only a room to pass through on their way to anywhere else. Unless that is, they were being called into it to eat a meal that someone else prepared. Jon seemed completely at ease in his culinary role, and thirty minutes later we were polishing off the last remnants of a surprisingly tasty dinner. I began to gather the dishes to take to the sink. "Why don't you go to the other room and relax while I clean this up?"

"Deal. That's one part of the plan I forgot to mention. Whoever cooks never has to clean up. Of course, in my college days that often meant I'd have to put up with looking at a pile of dirty dishes for days, until one of my roommates finally got around to washing them. Sometimes I just gave in and did them myself."

"Well, you won't have to worry about that with me. I can't stand to look at dirty dishes, or dirty anything, for that matter. I'm a bit of a neat freak."

"A neat freak. That's an interesting expression. Is that anything like a control freak?"

I laughed. "In a way, I guess. Except I don't really have a problem not being in control in every situation, except when it comes to tidiness. In fact, sometimes it's a relief to just follow someone else's lead. It's a lot less work that way."

He leaned against the kitchen counter and regarded me curiously. "You're an interesting person, Georgia Ayres. Just when I think I've figured you out, you say something that totally throws me off guard."

I had to move very close to where he was standing in order to get to the sink, and I found his nearness distracting. I tried to appear nonchalant as I waved him into the other room. "I'll just be a few minutes here. You can watch some TV if you want." His expression told me I hadn't fooled him for a minute. Luckily, he took the hint. A few seconds later I heard the sound of the television and I took a deep breath to release the tension I had been holding in ever since I first saw him sitting on my front steps. I told myself it was just because I was nervous about discussing the Belmont plan with him, but the truth was I felt that way every time I was around him.

I finished drying the last plate and hung the dish towel over the oven door handle, then went to join Jon in the den. The evening news was playing on the television, but it was falling onto deaf ears because both of the inhabitants of the room were sound asleep. Jon's head had fallen back onto the sofa cushions, and I could hear his breathing in quiet rhythm. Ebie had tucked herself snugly against his right thigh, and he had one arm braced protectively around her little body. The sight of the two of them looking so comfortable almost brought me to tears. There was just something so right about the scene, which both thrilled me and scared me at the same time.

Jon had looked so tired all night I didn't have the heart to wake him. I picked up a small throw I kept on the sofa and laid it gently over his side, being careful not to cover Ebie in the process. Neither one stirred. I stood for a moment taking in the scene. It filled my heart so completely I was reluctant to move away. I turned off the lights and made my way into the bedroom, shutting the door behind me. I wasn't sure I would be able to fall asleep. After all, this was the first time a man had spent the night since I'd moved into my apartment. Just before sleep claimed me, I smiled as it occurred to me that here, I was alone with a handsome, exciting, intriguing man, and Ebie was the one who ended up sleeping with him. Just my luck!

Chapter 19

The next morning, I was awakened by the smell of coffee. My eyes jerked open as the memory of my overnight guest came to mind. That guest was apparently wide-awake and in my kitchen this very moment, which meant I had to face him sooner rather than later. I groaned and considered pulling the covers over my head and hiding out until Jon finally gave up and left. But I realized I had an urgent need to visit the bathroom, which required me to leave the security of my bed. I stood and grabbed a robe from the hook on my bedroom door and tied it snugly around me. I ran my fingers through my sleep-ruffled hair and braced myself for what, and whom, I was about to face.

Jon was sitting at the kitchen table drinking coffee. He looked up with a smile. I waved a hand in his direction and quickly slipped into the bathroom. When I emerged a few minutes later he was standing at the kitchen counter pouring more coffee into his mug. He pulled a second mug from the cabinet. "I won't ask how you take your coffee since the answer is obvious from the lack of cream or sugar in your kitchen." He turned around and held the mug out to me with a smug grin.

"Thanks. I actually like it with milk, but I ran out and I haven't gotten around to buying more." I took a careful sip. "Umm. This is good. Did you put something different in it?"

"Cinnamon. It takes some of the bitterness out of the coffee."

"I have cinnamon?"

He chuckled at the look of surprise on my face and shook his head in wonderment. "Unless the jar marked cinnamon actually contains something else. Actually, given the sparseness of your food supply, I should have considered that possibility." I noticed his eyes move down to my feet then slowly make their way back up to my face. "Cute."

I looked down and felt my face grow hot as I realized I was not only wearing purple pajama bottoms with white sheep images showing below the hem of my robe, but I had also tucked my feet into my favorite pair of slippers made to look like tigers. I groaned and sat at the table, tucking my feet under the legs of my chair. "They're warm. I'm not used to having to worry about anyone else seeing them."

He sat in the chair opposite mine. "No need to apologize. You look adorable." His eyes locked onto mine. "Thanks for letting me crash here last night. I don't usually fall asleep in other people's apartments. That is unless I'm invited to." His look suggested that being invited to sleep over was not something completely uncommon for him.

I found myself bristling at the suggestion behind his comment. I knew, right from the start, there were a lot of differences between us. He was several years older, and obviously had a lot more worldly experience. But I didn't like to be reminded of those facts, especially when he was sitting in my kitchen, drinking my coffee, and looking as good as he did. I mean, HOW could he look as good as he did? He couldn't have slept very well, slumped over on my lumpy sofa. But his sleep tossed hair, unshaven face, and rumpled clothes only seemed to increase his attractiveness.

I suddenly felt like I couldn't sit still any longer. I stood and dumped the rest of my coffee in the sink. "I'm sorry but I have a lot of things to do today. Thank you for making coffee."

He frowned and gave me a puzzled look. "Did I say something to offend you? It suddenly feels like I'm getting the bum's rush".

"I'm not used to having a man sleep over, if that's what you mean. Even though it obviously meant nothing to you at all." My words came out harsher than I intended, and only increased my feelings of discomfort.

His eyes narrowed and his mouth formed a tight line as he continued to stare at me. "Maybe you're offended because I didn't try to take advantage of the situation." He shook his head. "Regardless of what you think of me, you need to know, that would never happen."

I was surprised at the hint of anger in his voice, and I wondered what it meant. Was he upset that I hadn't encouraged him to turn the evening into something more, or could he be angry that I might think he would force things in a direction I didn't want? Perhaps he sensed I didn't really know what I wanted from him or with him, and he was getting tired of my uncertainty. It also occurred to me he might not have any feelings for me in that way at all. He'd certainly been flirtatious during our encounters, but he'd barely kissed me after our dinner date. Maybe I just wasn't his type.

When I finished rinsing out my coffee mug, I turned to face him. "You're right. It would never happen. This thing between us, whatever it is, definitely isn't headed in that direction. I didn't mean to imply that I thought it was."

A frown formed on his face as he moved to stand in front of me. "Now *I'm* confused. You seem to be saying there's nothing between us, nor could there ever be anything between us. Am I missing something here?"

I shrugged. "Isn't that what you meant? That nothing else would ever happen? It's pretty clear you don't think of me in that way."

He shook his head and ran his hands through his hair as he turned away from me, pacing across the kitchen floor before turning back around to face me. "What are you talking about? Do you have any idea what control it took for me not to climb into bed with you last night, or wake you with a smoldering kiss this morning? Surely you can't be so naïve that you haven't noticed how attracted I am to you?" He crossed the few steps between us and placed his hands firmly on my shoulders. "The only reason I didn't do those things is I don't want this to be rushed. You're young, and I'm guessing inexperienced. I want to give you time to decide how you feel about me, about us. What I was trying to say is I'm not the kind of guy who tries to force his way into a woman's bed."

He was standing so close I could smell the coffee on his breath and see the dark stubble of beard that shadowed his face. I found myself wondering what it would feel like to rub my hand over the roughness of his cheeks; to taste the coffee on his lips, to give in to the urge to feel the heat from his body pressed against mine.

I stepped sideways so I could slip away from the pressure of his hands, but also so I could break the spell that threatened to send me down a path I wasn't sure I wanted to go. What good would it do to get involved with him? I didn't even know how long he planned to stay in Nashville. Once he was gone, it was unlikely he would remember me as anything more than a passing flirtation who helped to fill his time.

"I think it's best if we keep our focus on what matters here, which is trying to find a way to save *The Daily Courier*. That is, if you were serious about wanting that to happen."

He regarded me solemnly. "I wouldn't have said so if I didn't mean it." He sat his mug on the counter and turned to walk away. "I'll look into things from my end and get back to you. In the meantime, I suggest you avoid saying anything about this to anyone else. If word gets out about what we have in mind, we might find ourselves facing unforeseen roadblocks." He opened the door and started to walk out, but then turned back around to look at me. "As for the rest, you might want to spend some time figuring out what you want. I have no desire to play guessing games." He left my apartment, shutting the door firmly behind him.

Ebie pranced over to the closed door and mewed emphatically. I walked to her, bending to stroke her head. "I know. You didn't want him to go. Actually, I'm not sure I did either, but I guess I pretty well botched things up." I flopped on the sofa and rubbed my eyes with the palms of my hands. "What is *wrong* with me? I feel like I have all of these mixed emotions whirling around inside, and they end up causing me to say the dumbest things." I sighed heavily. It seemed I had two challenges in front of me. I wasn't sure which one I feared the most.

The next few days seemed to creep by. Luckily, I had a few assignments at the newspaper that occupied my attention and helped to pass the time. Ida phoned at the beginning of the week to tell me Mr. Bookman was still on board with our plan, and was just waiting for word from us about how to proceed. Unfortunately, I hadn't heard a word from Jon since he left my apartment, and I was wondering if my personal confusion had cooled his interest in our project. He asked me to trust him, which I was trying hard to do. But it wasn't easy, given that the clock was ticking away on any possibility of rescuing *The Daily Courier* from its previously defined fate.

By Friday, I was beginning to lose faith that Jon would call when a messenger showed up at my work with a letter from him. I tore open the envelope and quickly read the note inside. *Had to leave town suddenly. Everything looks good for the plan. Expect a call from my secretary later today with details. Jon Barnett.* I folded the piece of paper and tucked it carefully away inside my satchel, wondering why the message left me feeling unsettled. It seemed like good news when it came to the Belmont plan, but the cool, matter-of-fact tone reminded me how our last time together ended. "What do you expect, Georgia?" I asked myself. "You pushed him away, and now you want to know why he's keeping you at a distance."

I decided to place a call to Ida to let her know that things seemed to be moving forward. I suggested I come by her office to fill her in on the details. I gave her the excuse that I didn't want anyone else to overhear our conversation, but the truth was; I wanted to see her face when she read Jon's letter, to see if her reaction matched mine.

When I arrived at her office, I quickly described the conversation I had with Jon about our plans, intentionally leaving out the details of where the conversation took place, then handed her his note to read. She looked it over quickly and gave it back to me. "Well, that sounds promising, doesn't it?"

I nodded, although my frown must have betrayed my true feelings.

"Why don't you tell me what's really on your mind? I know you well enough by now to recognize when something's bothering you."

I sat in my usual spot across from her and slumped in the chair. "I'm afraid I botched things up with Jon. He was waiting for me at my apartment when I got home Friday night, and he ended up staying over. Not in that way!" I quickly added when I saw the look of surprise she gave me. "He fell asleep on the sofa with Ebie in his lap and I didn't have the heart to wake him. Everything was going great until I decided to practically chase him out the door the next morning." I shook my head mournfully. "The formal tone of his note makes me think he's decided to keep things totally professional between us."

Ida studied me carefully. "Isn't that what you want?"

I looked at her glumly. "That's the problem. I don't know how I feel about him or what I want to do about those feelings, if anything. He pretty much told me he expects me to figure it all out or he doesn't want to bother with me anymore."

She reached forward and patted my hand. "In my experience, when it comes to matters of the heart, it's best to keep things as simple as possible. Perhaps you are overcomplicating things with Jon. Why don't you apply your journalism training to figure out what you want, or don't want, from your relationship with him?"

I frowned in confusion. "You mean I should ask *who, what, when, where, why, and how?*"

She smiled. "Precisely! Lay it all out as straightforward as possible. It may help you clarify your feelings."

I considered her suggestion carefully. "I never would have thought of that. You think it would work?"

She smiled at me patiently. "I honestly have no idea. But it seems doing something is preferable to staying bogged down in the quandary you seem to be stuck in at the moment."

I nodded in response. *Why not try to lay things out as simply as she described?* It always worked for me when I was plotting out a story for the newspaper. Why shouldn't it work when I was trying to plot out the story of my life? "I'll give it a try. As you said, doing something feels a lot better than doing nothing."

She looked at me thoughtfully. "Regardless of what people say, change is not always for the best. But staying put can be just an excuse to avoid the unknown."

I stood to leave. "Thank you, Ida. You always help me regain my footing when I feel off-kilter." I started to walk to the door, but turned around and gave her a quick hug. "You are a true friend."

She returned my hug warmly, and I thought I could detect a faint shimmer of tears in her eyes as I turned to leave.

Chapter 20

Despite my initial concerns that our idea of relocating *The Daily Courier* to Belmont could ever really happen, the plan began to move ahead swiftly. In the week that followed my visit to Ida, the money was allocated to add a wing to the Mansion. Thomas Bookman succeeded in securing administrative support from the College to add faculty to the journalism program in order to accommodate the expected increase in enrollment. The publisher and editor of *The Daily Courier* was filled in on the plan to relocate offices and staff to the new site. A letter was received from the Barnett Corporation officially confirming their agreement to support the revitalization of *The Daily Courier*. The only thing missing was Jon. Of course, his presence was indirectly felt through the various forms of communication that transpired between his family's business and the Belmont administration. But he still had not returned to Nashville.

Perhaps it was a good thing I hadn't seen Jon since he left my apartment. Despite my intent to explore my feelings toward him, I was still putting off facing that challenge. Procrastination is a funny thing. It presents an effective roadblock against accomplishing what is most important, but it tricks us into believing the culprit is time. The truth is, time is rarely a factor when it comes to doing what needs to be done. It's just easier to blame our stalling on a lack of time, rather than admit we're afraid of confronting whatever it is we're choosing to delay. Sometimes it's a fear of failure, but just as often, it's a fear of beginning a task that leads to an uncertain ending. In my case, I was afraid of what I would discover about myself. On some level, most likely a deeply embedded one, I believed I had been effective in my life so far because I had succeeded in keeping my fears at a distance. Exploring those fears intentionally meant allowing them to rise to the surface. To be honest, the thought of doing that scared me to death.

I decided what I needed, in order to face the process of uncovering my true feelings about Jon and my feelings about myself, was moral support. That meant I had to convince Julie to join me in my pursuit of discovery. Being the great friend she is, she agreed without hesitation.

We decided to meet at my apartment after work on Friday. It never occurred to me to wonder why we always ended up at my place when hers was just as close and nearly as small as mine. I suspected it was because mine was adorned with a balcony, which had become our go-to spot since the first day I moved in.

Julie showed up carrying two cushions to use on my hard, wooden chairs, in anticipation of a long spell of sitting. My contribution was a thick notepad and pen, cheese and crackers, and a bottle of wine. I still wasn't much of a drinker, but I was hoping the alcohol would loosen the ties that kept my innermost feelings wrapped up. Since Jon suggested I improve my selection of food and drink, I had been making an effort to branch out from my usual choice of beer and chips.

The outside air was breezy, filled with the faint scent of rain predicted for later that night. It lent a pleasant coolness to what had been an unseasonably warm day for early March. We both sat quietly for a few minutes, sipping our wine and munching on the snacks. Ebie was prancing back and forth from one end of the balcony to the other, seemingly intent on following the activities of a squirrel hopping from branch to branch in a nearby tree. She had gained strength and size in the past few weeks, and I was a little worried she would decide to try to climb the railing in order to leap toward the squirrel. However, after watching her for a few minutes, I decided she seemed content to watch her prey from a distance.

I looked at Julie and found her staring at me. "What?" I asked.

"I'm been waiting to see if you're going to get this ball rolling or if I'm going to have to kick-start it for you."

I made a face at her and picked up the pen and paper. "I was just enjoying the breeze." I opened the notepad to the first page and wrote 5 W's and 1 H down the left side, then turned the page so she could see it.

Her eyes opened wide in surprise. "What is that supposed to be? Don't tell me you're going to try to figure out how you feel about Jon by using that old journalism technique?"

I frowned at her and laid the notepad in my lap. "It was Ida's idea. She said it would be best to approach things as simply as possible, and she suggested using the same approach I use when I'm working on a newspaper assignment."

Her face showed her doubt. "There is such a thing as being *too* simplistic." She threw her hands in the air and shrugged. "But what do I know? Let's try Ida's way first. If that doesn't work, we'll take another approach."

I chose a cracker and laid a piece of cheese on it before shoving it into my mouth. I munched away, studying the first letter. Julie leaned over to look at the page. "W. If I remember correctly, that stands for WHO. That should be an easy one to figure out." She leaned back in her chair and nibbled on a piece of cheese while I wrote Jon Barnett next to the W, then mulled over what else I was supposed to write. Beside his name, I added "newspaper publisher and owner." At the second W, I wrote WHAT. That one wasn't too hard to figure out either, since Jon made it clear he wanted me to decide *what* I wanted or didn't want from our relationship. I wrote *boyfriend* next to the second W. I had considered writing *friend* as a second option, but the truth was, if I were to continue to see him, I didn't believe either of us would be comfortable limiting our relationship to a platonic friendship.

The third W stood for WHEN. I took that to mean that if I wanted him to be my boyfriend, when did I want that to happen? This was starting to get harder. I realized I would have to go back up and tackle the answer to the second W before I could go any further. This was why I wanted Julie around. I held the page up for her to see, pointing at the WHAT. She glanced over at the page and seemed to contemplate her answer.

"First of all, he's a man. That's clearly *what* he is. Secondly, he's an older, more experienced man, which is maybe *what* you're afraid of, or does that fall under the *Why*"? She shook her head emphatically. "Forget I said that. What do you think of when you think of Jon Barnett?"

I chewed on the end of the pen as I considered her question. "Do you want me to rattle off a list of adjectives that I think describe him?"

She nodded. "Let's try that."

"Okay. Handsome. Exasperating. Confusing. Handsome. Intriguing. Puzzling. Did I say handsome?"

She chuckled at my obvious attempt at humor. "I think we're seeing a theme here. Physically, you're drawn to the guy. Beyond that, he keeps you guessing what he's all about. It's like a seesaw ride…you never know whether you're going to be on the up side, or the down. Sounds like a recipe for constant turmoil to me."

I considered what she said. "Maybe I wasn't totally fair in how I described him. Everything I said was true, but he has also given me some indication of a softer side. Like, the way he acts with Ebie, how he talks about his sister and her kids, and the way he looked so sad and vulnerable after the plan to shut down *The Daily Courier* was announced. It's like he's two different people; the one he is when his guard is down, and the one he was trained to be. Some things he said gave me the impression his father has been pretty tough on him his whole life. It's like he's worked hard at trying to meet his father's expectations, which has caused him to adopt an outside image of tough arrogance."

Julie took a careful sip of wine. "Okay. Now we're getting somewhere. It sounds like another couple of adjectives you've just described are: *contradictory* and *guarded*. The question is, do you think he wants to let his guard down around you to let you see his vulnerable side?"

I frowned at her question. "I'm not sure. He's made a couple of comments that lead me to believe he's aware of how he comes across. Maybe he doesn't want to be that way with me."

"Alright. What about the *When*? From what you've told me, you've been pushing him away every time he takes a step toward you. That doesn't sound like you're ready for a relationship with him. Maybe it really means you're afraid of the intensity of what you're feeling. The only guys I can remember you dating were—forgive my honesty—oddballs. Most of them were nice enough, but they all had some kind of quirkiness that kept them from quite fitting in anywhere. They were like puppies you took home to housetrain, then turned them lose when you got tired of how much work that took. The bottom line was, they seemed to need you a lot more than you needed them. Maybe what scares you about Jon is you think he's stronger than you. You're afraid if you give in to wanting him, that want will turn into need. That turns the tables on where you're used to being, and it exposes you to the possibility of getting hurt."

I looked at her with a mixture of surprise and admiration. "Are you sure you didn't go into the wrong profession? It seems to me you just did a fairly accurate job of analyzing my life so far."

She smiled shyly. "I guess that's what comes from being in therapy for years. The process can't help but rub off."

I looked at her in astonishment. "You never told me you were in therapy!"

"Not were, am. I started seeing someone shortly after we moved to Nashville. Believe it or not, I had a hard time adjusting to life here, and my parents were worried that if I didn't get the help I needed, I would flunk out of school. Therapy helped me have the confidence to do things I wasn't totally comfortable with." She looked at me pointedly. "Like, speak to a stranger in the school lunchroom and basically invite myself to eat with her."

Her revelation reminded me of our first meeting. I was shocked to learn that the confident manner in which she came across was the product of psychotherapy. "Why didn't you ever tell me about being in therapy? Were you worried it would make me think you were crazy or something?"

She looked down at the floor as she considered my question. "At first, I guess I thought it would brand me as some kind of nut. Later on, it just didn't seem important to mention. Being in therapy was just part of who I was; who I *am*. I got to the point where I didn't think of it as anything different than going to get a haircut. It was something I did to help me feel better about myself."

"Well, it certainly worked. I've always thought of you as one of the most well-adjusted people I've ever met. Maybe I should go see your therapist."

Her smile said she was both flattered by my description of her, and pleased at the idea that I would consider therapy as something I could benefit from. too.

"If you're interested, just let me know and I'll give you her number. In the meantime, let's get back to the task at hand. WHEN do you think you'll be ready to allow yourself to take a chance on love? That's what it really boils down to, doesn't it? This guy has plucked your heartstrings and it scares you."

I frowned at the truth in her statement. "Let's leave WHEN as a big question mark for now. Maybe if I go through the rest of the list, I'll be closer to giving you an answer." I looked down at the notepad. "WHERE. That brings up another problem. His home is in Washington, mine is in Nashville. He's never given me any indication that he'd be interested in moving here. I can't see myself uprooting to another state just because there's a possibility of something working out with him. So, where does that leave us?"

She nibbled thoughtfully on a cracker as she considered my question. "It seems the only thing you need to know for now is whether or not he's going to stay around Nashville long enough for you to figure out if there's any chance of a future together. What has he said about his plans?"

"He hasn't. He mentioned he leased his car because he didn't know how long he planned to stay here. After the *Courier's* relocation is finalized, I can't imagine he'd have any other reason to stay around."

"Sounds like you need to put a big star next to that W. Find out when he plans to leave Nashville. Then you'll have a better idea of whether the rest of these questions even need to be answered."

I looked at the list. All that was left was WHY and HOW. I realized Julie was right. There was no point in thinking about *why* I wanted to allow myself to be open to a relationship with him, or *how* that might transpire, unless he was going to be around long enough to allow it to happen. Once again, she seemed to have helped me get a clearer sense of what I needed to do. I closed the notepad and laid it on the table, picking up my mostly full wine glass. "You're right. I need to talk with him. But he hasn't called since he left my apartment. As far as I know, he still hasn't returned to Nashville. Maybe all of this was a wasted effort."

Julie gave me a sympathetic look. "It's hard to wait around for someone else to take the next step. Did it ever occur to you that you don't have to wait? It seems like he's given you every indication the next move is yours. Why don't you take things into your own hands?"

I sighed audibly. "I know you're right, but that's the last thing I feel like doing. Don't you think I could just wait a little longer?" I looked at her hopefully, but the firm line to her mouth told me her answer. "Okay, forget I asked that." I stood and stretched. "What would you say about us taking a walk? All of this heavy thinking has made me tired and I need to get the kinks out of my body."

She pushed up from her chair and twisted from side to side. "Sounds good to me. Maybe we can get in a few turns around the neighborhood before the rain starts." She nodded toward the sky, which had noticeably darkened since we first sat.

We carried our things inside and made our way to the door. As we were leaving, I reached over and squeezed her shoulder "Thanks."

She leaned into me and hugged me around the waist. "Anytime. I really hope things work out for you."

Chapter 21

I was walking through the newsroom a few days later when I saw Don Williams striding purposefully in my direction. He motioned for me to follow him. When we reached the front of the building, he opened the door and indicated I should step outside. As soon as we were both standing on the sidewalk in front of the building, he turned to me with his hands on his hips.

"You just couldn't leave well enough alone, could you? What did you think you were accomplishing by campaigning to save the *Courier*?"

His comments took me by surprise. I knew word had begun to leak out about the plan to relocate *The Daily Courier*, but I had no idea my name had been linked to the idea. I felt as if my heart had stopped. I searched for something to say to reassure him of my intentions. Unfortunately, before I could say anything, he moved closer and pointed a finger at my face.

"*The Daily Courier* was our only competition. With it out of the way, *The Nashville News* would have become the only source of news for Nashville. Do you have any idea what that would have meant for us? It would have secured the future of the paper, and along with it, the jobs of everyone on it. What you've done will completely shake things up, and not in a good way. But I imagine you didn't think about any of that when you were working your way into Barnett's favors. I can't help but wonder what you had to do to pull this off."

His angry tone and the insinuation that I had somehow singlehandedly managed to save *The Daily Courier*, and harm the future of *The Nashville News,* shocked me to my core and left me speechless. Not only was it outlandish to think I could have wielded that much power if I wanted to, I found his suggestion that I may have been cozying up to Jon in order to manipulate the future of *The Daily Courier* to be personally insulting.

He turned on his heel and quickly walked back towards the entrance to the building, jerking the door open before turning back to look at me once more. "You're fired. Those orders come from the big boss himself. He told me to tell you that he doesn't want to see your face around here anymore. You've got until the end of the day to clear your things out." He slammed the door behind him, leaving me standing alone with my mouth hanging open.

I felt as shell-shocked as if someone had just placed an explosive device at my feet and detonated it. My head was spinning and I felt like I would be sick. I leaned against the wall of the building and tried to catch my breath. *Fired*? Could he have said that? I knew he had, but it still didn't make sense to me. How had I gone from trying to do something I thought would help the newspaper industry in general, to being branded as a traitor to my own paper?

I wasn't sure what to do next. I didn't want to go back inside the building because it was quite likely my fellow reporters would view me with the same disdain Don Williams had. Luckily, I had my work satchel and purse with me because Don had caught me just as I arrived. I walked quickly to the parking lot and fished my car keys out of my purse. My hand was shaking so much I had to use my other hand to hold the key steady enough to get it into the lock. Once inside, I leaned my forehead on the steering wheel and let the tears flow down my face.

I was still in that position, trying to collect myself enough to drive home, when I heard a tap on the car window. I lifted my head to find Seymour Collins looking in at me. Seymour was assigned to the city beat and his desk was next to mine. I never really thought of him as a friend, but he had at least been friendly to me when most of the other reporters were treating me like I harbored a communicable disease. His expression looked like a mixture of sympathy and pity, so I rolled the window down slowly.

"Hey," he said. "I heard Don and Ralph talking early this morning. When I saw Don usher you out, I had a feeling things hadn't gone too well for you." He seemed to be studying my tear streaked face and reddened eyes. "I guess I was right. Look. If you want, I can get your things and bring them out to you. Or, better yet, I could drop them by your apartment later."

His offer tempted me. I really didn't want to spend another minute near the building, in case someone else wandered by and saw me. "Thanks. That's really nice of you. Do you think you could just put everything in a box and let me come by for it sometime tomorrow? I could call you first so you could bring them outside."

He seemed to hesitate before answering. "I guess that'll work. Are you sure you don't want me to bring them over later? We could have a drink or something."

His suggestion made a little alarm go off in my gut. I shook my head and began to roll up the window. "On second thought, why don't you just leave everything where it is? I'll figure out how to get them."

His face seemed to change from friendly to scornful. "If you say so. You shouldn't be so picky. We could have had a good time together."

His words confirmed my fears. I rolled the window up the rest of the way and started the car. As I pulled out of the parking lot, I glanced in my rear-view window to see him still standing in the same spot I left him, his hands jammed deep into his pockets and a scowl twisting his face. *What the hell is going on?* I thought.

Things seemed to have spun out of control and I didn't know what to do about it.

I was about to head for home when it occurred to me Ida might know something that could help explain what was happening in my life. I drove the few blocks to the Stahlman building, parked the car, and rode the elevator up to her floor. The door to the MHC was standing open, but I knocked quietly on the doorframe before entering. I spotted her standing at a window looking out, but her eyes didn't seem to be focused on anything in particular. When I knocked a second time, she turned to look at me. The worried expression on her face only seemed to deepen as she saw me.

"Oh, Georgia. I'm so glad it's you. I've been trying to think how to tell you what has happened." She gave me a long look. "But it appears that someone may have beaten me to it. Why don't you sit down so we can talk?"

I took a seat in my usual chair and described my conversation with Don, as well as the odd interaction with Seymour. Ida listened quietly, but the expression on her face betrayed the obvious distress she was feeling. When I finished, she leaned back heavily in her chair and shook her head.

"It's even worse than I imagined. I'm so sorry you had to go through all of that."

I looked at her mournfully. "You said you were trying to think how to tell me what happened. Can you explain what this is all about? It doesn't make any sense to me."

She paused for a moment as if to gather her thoughts. "After we met with Thomas the other day, he took it upon himself to phone Ralph Stein." I looked at her with alarm. "I know. I was as surprised as you are. But I have to believe that his intentions were good. He said he wanted to make sure Mr. Stein wouldn't attempt to interfere with our plans. He knew him from the days when he was working as a string reporter on *The Daily Courier*. On more than one occasion, Ralph Stein had tried to convince him to leave *The Daily Courier* to become a reporter for *The Nashville News*. As you have no doubt experienced, very little goes on around there that escapes Mr. Stein's attention, so he was aware of Thomas' frustrations. Because of that, Thomas felt they were on good enough terms to speak with him candidly. I'm afraid he was tricked, Georgia. At first, Mr. Stein gave him the impression he was keen on the idea, and he used that as leverage to get Thomas to provide him with the details regarding how the plan came about. Once he had all the information he needed, he flew into a rage and began to throw out all sorts of accusations. Thomas said he tried to calm him. He even tried to convince him the whole idea was the result of Jon Barnett's earlier actions. Mr. Stein insisted on believing you had been working behind the scenes for weeks to pull this off. Nothing Thomas said could convince him otherwise."

I was stunned. What I heard made me realize the situation was even worse than I imagined. "I don't know what to be more upset about; that he may manage to call a halt to our plans, or that he has pegged me as the villain."

She looked at me sympathetically. "I know things seem bad now, but if we assume that Ralph Stein has won this battle, we may as well kill the plan ourselves."

Her statement made no sense to me. "But isn't that exactly what has happened? Surely, we don't have a chance of pulling this off, now that he's caught wind of it."

She patted my knee, and I noticed her mouth had taken on the determined look I had come to recognize. She was brewing up a scheme of some sort. "My aunt used to say, 'It's not over till it's over'. I think that certainly applies to this situation. Ralph Stein may hold all the cards when it comes to running his newspaper, but if he thinks he can bully his way into making us turn on our heels and run away, he's in for a surprise." She stood and began to gather her things. "Come on, Georgia. We have a war to win." The confident look on her face lifted my spirits, but I was a long way from sharing in her certainty. I grabbed my purse and followed her out the door.

Chapter 22

When Ida and I left her office, we hopped into *Tweedledee* and headed straight for the Belmont campus. On the way there, Ida described what she had in mind, which basically amounted to gathering our resources and trying to push our plan into high gear. Since our resources added up to Ida's money and Thomas' influence, gathering them was a simple matter of making a bank transfer, securing the Belmont administration's signature on the contract that spelled out the plan to relocate the *Courier*. Apparently, Ida and Thomas had made sure both of those matters were taken care of immediately after it had become clear that Ralph Stein was not in favor of the plan. That only left one thing still out of order—the Barnett family's official stamp of approval, and Jon Barnett was still absent and unaccounted for.

Thomas' office was in its usual state of disarray when we arrived. Books and papers were stacked and scattered on every possible surface in what looked like utter chaos. His secretary, Mrs. Stayhill, informed us Thomas was just finishing teaching a class, so we pushed aside some of the stacks and settled down to wait. He arrived about ten minutes later, trailed by two students who seemed eager to catch some final words from their professor.

When he spotted us, he shooed them away and sat wearily at his desk.

"Was I ever that young?" He ran his fingers through his hair in an unsuccessful attempt to flatten out the cowlick that stuck up at odd angles on the top of his head. He had no sooner sat than he jumped up again. "Coffee?" He picked up a mug and looked at us questioningly. I looked at Ida, who shook her head.

"No thank you, Thomas. I'm afraid we're here with some unpleasant news." She proceeded to describe the interaction I had with Ralph Stein, discretely leaving out the details about Seymour's insinuation. Thomas listened intently, nodding when she finished.

"I was afraid something like that would happen." He looked at me sympathetically. "I'm so sorry, Georgia. You didn't deserve that. I wish I could turn back the clock and reverse my decision to talk to Ralph. I'm afraid I was caught off-guard by his reaction, and didn't handle it very well. It's terrible you were put in the middle of this, and had to lose your job as a result. Maybe I can, at least, remedy that. I'm sure I can find a position for you here temporarily. The new program is up and running, it would be a perfect fit for you to become one of our permanent instructor/reporters."

I looked at him with surprise. "Are you sure? I haven't really thought about what I'm going to do next, but that sounds great."

He smiled and walked to his office door. "Why don't I get Mrs. Stayhill to start the paperwork right now? I'm afraid we can't pay you much to begin with, but at least it should be close to what a fledgling reporter makes." He motioned for me to follow him. "In the meantime, Ida and I will put our heads together about the rest of it."

A half hour later, the documents had been completed that would enable me to start work with the journalism program at Belmont. As I understood it, my position would basically place me as an assistant to Thomas, with responsibilities ranging from doing research, grading papers, to running errands. That was fine with me. Everything had happened so fast I really hadn't had time to let it all sink in. That was probably just as well, because I was sure as soon as I thought through everything that had transpired, it would hit me hard. It was a great relief not to have to figure out how I was going to replace the income I lost at *The Nashville News*. But it would take a lot longer to replace the loss of my self-esteem.

I returned to Thomas' office to find him deep in conversation with Ida, their heads bent toward each other as they peered at a piece of paper on the desk between them. They both looked up with a smile as I walked in.

Ida was the first to speak. "Great news, Georgia. The Barnett family is sending the papers we need to confirm their support for the relocation of *The Daily Courier*. They should come through on the tele-copier in the Administration office within the hour. It seems everything is finally in order."

I looked from her to Thomas. "That's it? You mean it's actually going to work out?"

Both of them laughed at my obvious surprise. "It appears so," Thomas said. "Of course, there's still a lot to do to finalize the actual arrangements, but I'd say things are moving quickly in the right direction."

I wanted to ask how they knew the papers were being sent and whether Jon had anything to do with it, but I was hesitant to speak of him. Luckily for me, Ida's radar was still working.

"Apparently, when Jon returned home, he called an immediate meeting of the Barnett Corporation's Board of Directors and pretty much insisted they support our plan." She explained. "We just got off the phone with him when you walked in. As I understand it, Jon basically told them if they didn't go along with the relocation, he would tender his resignation immediately. I don't know if he was bluffing, but his threat seemed to work." She smiled. "He also mentioned he'll be heading back to Nashville soon, and he plans to stay here, at least until everything involving the *Courier's* move is in order."

I was having trouble taking in everything I was hearing. The Barnett Corporation was supporting our plan. Jon had called. He was coming back to Nashville, and staying around for a while. On top of everything else, I had a new job. I shook my head in wonder. "That's amazing. I don't know how you pulled it off, but it sounds like everything is working out the way we hoped it would."

Thomas walked over to me, extending his hand in my direction. "*We* pulled it off. None of this would have happened if you hadn't come up with the idea to start with. Welcome to the team, Georgia!" I accepted his offered hand and shook it numbly. "Thanks." I looked from him to Ida and back again. They were both grinning broadly and I found myself caught up their delight. "I guess I should call you 'Boss' now, or is 'Professor Bookman' more appropriate?"

Thomas looked at me with a wide-eyed expression before erupting in laughter. His laugh seemed to burst forth from his chest before it rolled over me in waves. His eyes were squeezed shut to barely hold back the tears of delight that threatened to spill over his cheeks. He was bent, doubled-over from the waist, and his hair kept flopping down over his forehead. Finally, he straightened, and cleared his throat in an obvious effort to get control over his laughter. I noticed his blue eyes appeared deeper in contrast to the red tint that came over his face. The sunlight that seeped in through the windows illuminated the hints of red in his hair, which he unsuccessfully attempted to push off his forehead. His whole appearance, not to mention the unbridled response my question provoked, made me imagine what he must have been like as a young boy. The image was not altogether unattractive.

He lifted a glass from his desk and took a deep drink of water. "I'm sorry, Georgia. I don't know why that struck me as so funny. I guess I've been building up a lot of tension wondering how all of this was going to work out. Your question just gave me an excuse to let it loose." He cleared his throat and set the glass down. "Please, just call me Thomas. I've never been one for unnecessary formalities."

He stood for a moment and seemed to try to collect his bearings before looking up once again with a grin. He dug his hands into his pockets and allowed his gaze to move from Ida to me and back again. Finally, he spoke. "I think this is cause for a celebration. I have a couple more classes to teach, and some appointments to keep this afternoon. But tonight, I'm going to treat you two ladies to the finest steak Nashville has to offer."

Ida had been unusually quiet throughout Thomas' giddy outburst. I glanced at her to see how she would respond to his invitation and was surprised to find her gazing off into space. Her face gave no indication what she was thinking, but I had the impression she was deep in thought about something. She must have sensed me staring at her because she suddenly seemed to pull herself up from wherever her thoughts had taken her and smiled at him warmly. "That sounds wonderful, Thomas, but if you don't mind, I'd like to take a rain check on that offer. I'm afraid I'm a bit tired. All the excitement, I guess. Georgia? Perhaps you'd like to join Thomas."

I had the oddest feeling there was some hidden reason for Ida's bowing out on dinner, but I was just too tired from all of the drama of the day to give it much thought. I shook my head in response. "I'm afraid I have to say no, too. I have to find a way to get my things from the newspaper office, then get ready to start my new job. I assume you want me to start tomorrow, Thomas?"

A look of disappointment crossed his face briefly before it was replaced by his customary grin. "No problem. Let's put dinner on hold for now and we'll all go out for that steak another time. As far as work goes, tomorrow would be great for you to start, but I thought you might like to take a day or two off before diving into a new job."

His offer came as a relief. I really didn't feel up to making such an abrupt change in my life without a little time to process everything that had happened. Yet, I didn't want to start off on the wrong foot in my new job. His invitation seemed quite sincere. In fact, I had the impression that Thomas Bookman was a person who could be counted on to say exactly what he was thinking at any given moment.

I nodded my agreement. "Maybe that would be best, if you're sure it's not an imposition. I could use a little time to let all of this sink in. "

He nodded. "Why don't you take the weekend and make a fresh start of it on Monday morning, say 9 o'clock? I'm usually here earlier than that, but nothing else gets going until around that time. Oh, one more thing. Let me take care of getting your things from the news office. I can imagine it wouldn't be very comfortable for you to go back in there right now. Since I was mostly to blame for the way things went down, it's the least I can do."

His offer was incredibly kind and I was more than a little relieved to accept it. I looked at Ida, who was nodding in agreement. "I think that's a fine idea, Thomas. Perhaps you can drop off Georgia's things to her over the weekend."

I looked at her questioningly, but she only offered me an innocent smile in return. "Okay," I said hesitantly. "If you're sure that's alright. Let me give you my phone number and you can call me when you want to bring the things over."

He waved his hand as I started to take out a pen to write down my number. "That won't be necessary. I can get it from my secretary. Why don't you take Ida home now? She must be very tired. I've never known her to turn down a steak dinner before." He looked at her pointedly.

Ida stood and shrugged. "Comes with the age, I suspect. Georgia? I'm ready if you are." She began to walk out the door. I jumped up quickly and followed her after thanking Thomas one more time.

When we reached the sidewalk, I took her arm by the elbow to get her attention. "Is there something going on that you're not telling me about? You seem to be preoccupied about something. You practically forced Thomas into agreeing to help me get my things from the office."

147

She waved off my question. "Nonsense. I just have a bit of a headache, which makes me feel tired, so I didn't feel up to going out to dinner. As for the other, I knew he'd be working tomorrow so it made perfect sense for him to bring your things to you over the weekend." She stopped walking and turned to face me. "I'm so glad you and Thomas will be working together. He can be a wonderful friend to have." She squeezed my hand firmly and resumed walking toward the car.

I stood for a moment in confusion before hurrying to catch up with her. There was definitely something going on, but I could tell by the firm set to her face I wasn't going to find out what it was until she was ready to tell me.

When we reached her house, she turned down my offer to walk her to the door, instead sending me off with a slight flutter of her fingers. I noticed she seemed to be moving slower than usual, which made me wonder if her excuse of being too tired to accept Thomas' dinner offer had been the truth after all.

When I finally walked in the door of my apartment, I felt so exhausted I barely made it to the sofa before collapsing. I kicked off my shoes and let my bags drop to the floor then turned sideways to lay my head on the cushion at one end. I was aware of Ebie jumping on my side before settling herself somewhat precariously along my hip. Just before sleep claimed me, the image of Thomas laughing hilariously flashed across my mind. The memory made me smile, and my last thought was how unusual it was to meet someone so open with his feelings. That brought to mind the image of Jon, who was as different from Thomas as two people could possibly be.

Chapter 23

True to his word, Thomas called on Friday afternoon to say he had picked up my things from my cubicle at the *News* and would drop them off around noon on Saturday. At ten o'clock on Saturday morning, I found myself scurrying around my apartment, picking up clothes, magazines, and various items I had allowed to accumulate over the past few days. Truth be told, I had done very little, other than move from my bed to the couch since returning home on Wednesday. It wasn't like me to let things get even a little disorderly. I viewed the assorted clutter with disdain, as if it was a constant reminder of my state of mind. I was still feeling the sting of being fired, and the added insult of the insinuations about my private life that both Don and Seymour had suggested. My *mostly non-existent private life,* I thought. There was a cruel irony that what existed only as a distant fantasy in my mind should have been called into question by anyone, especially two people who knew so little about me.

I finally managed to put my apartment back into some semblance of order and finished tidying up my own appearance when I heard a car door slam on the street outside. The balcony doors were open to allow a little of the warm breeze to enter my apartment. I peeked over the railing expecting to see Thomas and was surprised, instead, to see Jon striding purposefully toward my building. The lump in my throat, which always seemed to appear when he was nearby, caused me to swallow deeply. I ran my hands through my hair, hoping some of its defiant unruliness would be tamed, and waited for the sound of his knock.

When I opened the door, I was surprised to see he still looked as tired as the last time I had seen him. But the stony gaze he had given me when he left my apartment in anger was replaced by a look that, while not warm, was at least cordial.

"Hello, Georgia. I hoped I'd find you at home."

"Jon. I'm surprised to see you. Ida told me you'd be heading back to Nashville, but I didn't know it would be this soon." I stepped backward to open the door wider. "Do you want to come in?"

"If that would be alright. I was hoping we could talk."

He stepped inside and glanced around the room as if he couldn't figure out what to do next. I wasn't used to this more reserved version of Jon, and his hesitation threw me off-guard. "Do you want to sit? I could make some coffee."

"Just some water, if you don't mind." He walked toward the sofa and sat heavily. True to form, Ebie sensed his presence and pounced onto his lap, turning in a circle before settling down with a contented purr. I quickly filled two glasses from a pitcher of water I kept in the refrigerator and carried them into the living room. Jon took a sip, then cleared his throat. "I've been thinking for a long time about what I want to say to you, and I don't just mean since the last time I saw you. There are some things I've wanted to say since the first time we met at that god-awful Ball. Do you remember how awkward our first meeting was? All I could think about was how beautiful you looked…beautiful, yet terribly uncomfortable, and how I wanted to say something to make you feel better. But, as usual, all I ended up doing was insulting you and storming away." He shook his head and looked at the floor. "I'm surprised you even agreed to see me again after that."

I thought back to the night he was referring to. It was true; he had behaved very rudely to me at the end. So much so that seeing him again was the last thing I wanted to do. But I also remembered the flattering way he paid attention to me at the beginning of our encounter, and the unique gift he sent me at work, as an apology. Remembering it made me smile all over again.

"Let's just say you have a way of both pushing me away and pulling me back at the same time. I have to admit; your connection with the newspaper business, and the mystery of why you were in Nashville, caught the attention of my editor. Truthfully, it was his suggestion that I see you again. I guess he hoped I would find out what you were up to."

I expected him to either become irritated at what I revealed, or to at least express some degree of surprise. Instead, he just stared at me calmly. "I knew. Or at least, I suspected what was going on. But to be honest, it didn't matter. I wanted to get to know you. If having you spy on me was the only way it was going to happen, then I was willing to deal with that. Anyway, it seems the tables got turned on Ralph Stein. I'm sure by now he's regretting the day he insisted you continue to see me."

I nodded grimly. "No, I don't suspect he's thrilled by the way things turned out with *The Daily Courier*. He sure didn't waste any time taking it out on me."

He looked at me with surprise. "What do you mean?"

"He fired me. Not directly, but he had Don do it. Apparently, they're both convinced that everything that happened to change the plans for the *Courier* was due to a well-executed and devious plan I cooked up since I first met you. Don even went so far as to suggest that I have been trying to manipulate you into going along with the plan. He blindsided me with his accusations a few days ago in the street outside the *News*. He basically told me not to show my face around there anymore. I didn't even have the nerve to go inside to collect my personal things."

He shook his head in disbelief. "That's absurd. It sounds like they were looking for a scapegoat and saw you as an easy target. Do you want me to talk to them? I might be able to get you your job back."

I shook my head emphatically. "NO! There's no way I would feel comfortable working there again. And luckily, I don't have to. I've been hired by Thomas Bookman to work at Belmont College. I'll just be his assistant to start, but once *The Daily Courier* has moved there, I'll be involved in the production and educational side of things. Thomas was really great at coming to my rescue as soon as he heard what had happened."

His eyes narrowed as I spoke. "Are you sure he isn't just trying to take advantage of a bad situation?"

I was puzzled by the tone of suspicion in his question. Surely, he wasn't implying there was some ulterior motive in Thomas' hiring me. "He was just being nice. He also felt pretty guilty that I lost my job. Apparently, he was the one who made Mr. Stein aware of our plans." Jon's jaw tightened. "It's not what you think! He didn't do it intentionally. He knew him from when he used to work at the *Courier*, and he thought he could be upfront with him. Obviously, he didn't know Ralph Stein as well as he thought he did."

Jon shook his head and stood. "I still don't like the idea of him swooping in and rescuing you. Maybe I should have a talk with this Thomas Bookman. Find out what he's up to."

I was a little embarrassed to realize I had been taking pleasure in his faintly disguised show of jealousy. I had to struggle to control my expression before he caught on. Just as I was about to protest further about Thomas' intentions, I remembered he was on his way to my apartment at that very moment. In fact, he was already late. I was trying to decide whether Jon and I could make a quick exit in order to avoid what could be an awkward encounter, when I heard a knock on my door. Jon looked at me questioningly.

"I just remembered that Thomas offered to pick up my things from the *News* and bring them over here. That must be him now."

He folded his arms across his chest and turned to face the door. "Good. That'll give me the chance to check this guy out."

"Please don't make a scene. I promise you; he's just trying to be helpful." His face was sternly serious, which I had come to realize usually meant there was a storm brewing beneath the surface of his misleadingly calm exterior.

With a sigh, I walked over and opened my door. Thomas' arms were empty. I looked past him to see if he had left my things on the floor in the hallway, but there was nothing there. Thomas' face looked haggard.

"I'm sorry I don't have your things. I promise you I will still bring them to you, but something happened last night that prevented me from going to the newspaper."

There was something in the tone of his voice that scared me, and I quickly stepped aside to let him enter my apartment. He stopped just inside the door as he noticed Jon. The two men stared at each other without speaking.

"Thomas, this is Jon Barnett. You've probably spoken on the phone but I don't believe the two of you have actually met." Thomas seemed to collect himself as he stepped forward with an outstretched hand.

"Barnett. Yes. We spoke the other day. It's good to put a face to the voice."

I was relieved to see that Jon accepted his offered handshake, somewhat stiffly, but without hesitation.

"Bookman. Thank you for helping pull together the support of the Belmont administration for the relocation of *The Daily Courier*."

Thomas nodded grimly. "It was a team effort." He turned to look at me. "But I'm afraid I have some unfortunate news about one of the members of our team. I've just come from St. Thomas Hospital. Ida Hood was rushed there last night. One of her neighbors stopped by to return a dish and noticed her speech was slurred. Luckily, she called an ambulance and they rushed her to the hospital. The doctors think she may have suffered a stroke. I only found out about it because I have a nurse friend who works in the ER at St. Thomas. She happened to be on duty when Ida was brought in. She'd heard me talk about her often, so when she heard the name, she called me right away."

A sound escaped my throat that I barely recognized as coming from me. I wrapped my arms around my midsection as if to hold in my pain and looked from one man to the other. "How is this possible? We just saw her two days ago." I suddenly remembered how she had turned down the celebratory dinner Thomas offered with a plea of being tired, and how her shoulders seemed to slump more than usual as she walked from my car to her front door. Maybe if I had been less wrapped up in my own problems, I could have insisted on staying with her awhile. Or at least, called her later to see how she was feeling. Instead, I made it all about me. I even entertained the thought that her suggestion of being tired was all a ploy to play matchmaker between Thomas and me. *How silly I was, and how stupid, to allow myself to forget her age.*

I looked at Thomas and realized what I had taken for tiredness was really the reflection of the pain he had to be feeling. He had known Ida a lot longer than I, so I could only guess at how worried he must be. "What did the doctors say? Is she going to be alright?"

"I didn't actually get to talk to the medical staff. They're not allowed to discuss her situation with anyone except immediate family. I placed a call to her niece, Beth, in New York. She plans to fly down here later today. Once she has a chance to talk to the doctors we should know more." He cleared his throat and looked at the floor. "It doesn't sound good. My friend was able to glance at her chart before they moved her out of the ER. Apparently, she's had what they call a hemorrhagic stroke, which causes bleeding inside her brain. It's pretty rare, but it's the result of a genetic defect. I'm afraid I don't know much more about it than that, but my friend said she'd see what she could find out about Ida's case and let me know as soon as possible."

I felt as if the bottom had just dropped out of my world. I thought losing my job was bad, but the prospect of losing my friend; a friend who had become very special to me in a short period of time, made what had happened at work seem suddenly unimportant. "I'd like to see her. Will you take me to her?"

Jon stepped toward me and put an arm around my shoulders. "I'll drive you." He looked pointedly at Thomas. "Just tell us what room she's in."

Thomas shook his head at Jon and turned to face me again. "I'm afraid you can't see her, at least not yet. They still have her in the ICU. Hopefully, by the time her niece arrives, they will have been able to move her to a regular room." Sadness was etched onto his face. "I'm sorry to have to tell you all this, but I knew you'd want to know, and I didn't feel right telling you over the phone."

I nodded. "No. That would have been worse. I'm glad you told me personally. I just feel so helpless. Like I need to do something for her, but I can't figure out what to do."

He nodded his understanding. "I feel the same way. It's terrible knowing someone you care about is going through something so horrible, and there's not a damn thing you can do about it." His hair flopped over his forehead again, and he pushed it back absentmindedly. "I promise I'll let you know as soon as I hear anything."

The tears had begun to fall down my cheeks, as the enormity of what had happened began to sink in. I attempted to wipe them away with the sleeve of my shirt. "I just can't believe this. She was so strong and vibrant. How could this happen to her?"

Jon's arm was still around my shoulders and I could feel its gentle squeeze as I fought to gain control of my emotions. Thomas glanced at Jon, then back at me. His face seemed to suddenly register an awareness of our closeness, but I couldn't tell what he thought about it. He took a step away from us and shoved his hands into his pockets. "I'd better be going." He walked to the door but turned back. "She really cares about you, you know. She told me you were like the daughter she wished she'd had."

His words shook me to the core. I had to fight to keep from falling apart in a crying heap. "I love her. She's helped me more than she could possibly realize. I just hope I get a chance to tell her."

His eyes reflected his understanding. "She knows." He opened the door and walked out.

I suddenly felt as if all of the strength had left my body and I leaned into Jon. He wrapped both arms around me and led me to the couch. "You need to lie down. Why don't you try to rest a while? Then I'll get you something to eat."

I nodded numbly, although my stomach clinched at the idea of putting anything in it. I allowed him to remove my shoes and lift my legs onto the couch. He left the room for a minute, returning with a pillow and blanket from my bed. He laid the blanket carefully over me then scooted in next to me, placing my head on his pillow-covered lap. "I'm going to be right here. Rest for a while. Everything's going to be okay."

His last words stayed in my mind as I attempted to fall asleep. I wanted to believe what he said was true, but I had a sinking feeling it wasn't going to be okay. This was one time I wouldn't mind being wrong.

Chapter 24

I awoke sometime during the night and was surprised to find that, true to his word, Jon was still lying slumped over on the couch next to me. I sat up stiffly and glanced around the room. There was a faint light coming from the kitchen that Jon must have left on intentionally. I could just make out the numerals on the clock that read 1:15 A.M. I stood carefully and tried to stretch the kinks out of my back. My sofa was not designed for sleeping, and the crunched-up posture I had folded myself into left me stiff and sore. I walked to the balcony window and gazed out into the darkness. There was a sliver of a moon showing just above the trees, which gave the landscape a faint glow. I could see a gentle breeze blowing, so I carefully opened the balcony door and stepped outside. The night air held the slight chill common for an early, spring night. I wrapped my arms tightly around myself and gazed out at the darkness. Thoughts of Ida filled my mind. I could feel the tears begin to well up again as I imagined my friend alone in her hospital bed. I couldn't believe how drastically things had changed in just a few days. If I ever doubted the uncertain nature of life, those doubts had been dashed with a suddenness that was almost palpable in its ferocity. Her life could be hanging on the brink, and that realization made every other concern feel mundane and petty.

I looked up at the sky and offered a silent prayer for her recovery. A cloud slid over the moon temporarily blocking its light, which caused me to shiver as if I had just been given a foreboding message in response to my prayer.

"You must be cold." I hadn't heard Jon step onto the balcony beside me, but I welcomed the warmth of the blanket he wrapped around my shoulders, and the deeper warmth as he pressed his body against my back and enclosed me snugly in his arms.

"I was just thinking of Ida."

I could feel his silent strength as his arms held me a little more firmly. "We have to hope for the best. She's one of the strongest women I've ever met. If anyone can beat this thing, she can."

My heart remained uncertain. "I hope so, but I'm really worried about her."

Jon turned me around to face him, shifting the blanket so it enclosed the two of us in its warmth. "Just remember; you don't have to go through this alone. I'm here, and I don't plan to go anywhere."

I looked up at him and noticed the moonlight bathing his face in a soft glow. The heaviness in my heart lifted as it filled with the realization of what he said. "I'm glad you're here." I lifted my face toward him and pushed up onto my toes so I could plant a kiss. His lips were soft and surprisingly warm, and I felt the kiss deepen as he responded to me. His hands slipped beneath the blanket and sought the warmth of my skin through the cotton shirt I wore. He groaned softly and pulled back to gaze at me.

"I don't want to stop." His eyes seemed to deepen as he looked at me.

"Then don't," I replied.

His eyes widened as a faint smile curved his lips. "Are you sure?

"Stop talking and kiss me."

He pulled me tighter against him and leaned down to press his lips firmly against mine. I felt as if he was drinking me in, and the sensation had me reeling with a combination of lightheadedness and passion. He lifted me into his arms and carried me into my bedroom. He laid me down gently on the bed and began to unbutton his shirt. I reached up a hand to stop him. "I need to tell you something." He dropped his hands and looked at me with interest. "I've never been with a man before. I mean, I have, sort of, but not totally."

He sat on the bed beside me and studied me carefully. "Are you saying what I think you are? That this will be your first time?"

I answered with a nod and an apologetic lift of my shoulders. He shifted on the bed and seemed to consider what I said. "Okay. I have to admit, I hadn't anticipated that. It's been a long time since I was with someone who said those words to me. I guess I forgot our age difference." He shook his head and seemed to withdraw into himself. His sudden distance scared me, and I realized I needed to do something to pull him back from wherever he had gone. I placed my hand gently on his arm.

"It's okay. I want to be with you, Jon. I want to share this with you. I felt I owed it to you to let you know, but it doesn't change how I feel about being with you."

His eyes sparked with passion, but I could still sense he was holding back. I pulled on his arm so he was lying beside me. "I don't want to hurt you, Georgia. Not just physically, but emotionally, too. You've been through some difficult times lately, and the news about Ida has given you quite a shock. If you add all of that to what you've just told me, it suggests that what we were about to do may not be such a good idea." He caressed the side of my face and looked deep into my eyes. "You know how I feel. I may have been a little slow to tell you, but surely you could sense my interest in you a long time before I got around to saying anything. I'm just not so sure you know what you want. We never did have that conversation you know." His hand moved from my face to make a painstakingly slow descent along the curve of my neck to my shoulder and down the length of my arm. It felt like everywhere he touched was on fire, and I shuddered, in spite of the heat that his touch was producing. "Are you cold?" he asked, pulling the blanket up from where it had landed on the bed.

I answered by reaching up to finish unbuttoning his shirt. "Your touch makes me shiver, but not with cold. The only way you can hurt me is by leaving me lying here by myself." He placed his hands on each side of my face and kissed me hungrily. We gazed into each other's eyes for a minute, then he began to carefully undo the buttons on my blouse, his fingers stroking my skin as it was slowly exposed. When he had finally removed my blouse, he gazed down at me with an admiring look. "You're beautiful, you know. Even more than I imagined." He leaned down to caress my skin with his lips. Each spot he touched sent me spiraling deeper into a tingling passion unlike anything I had experienced before.

I reached up to slip his shirt off his shoulders. "Take this off. I want to see you, too."

He sat up and removed his shirt, tossing it on the floor before carefully laying down beside me with his head propped up with one hand. "Let's take this slow. I want your first time to be special."

I turned to face him allowing my gaze to take in the width of his shoulders and the powerful looking biceps that seemed to pulsate as he reached to caress my hip. I stretched my hand out to stroke his chest, allowing my fingers to outline the curves and angles there. His skin was surprisingly soft over the firmness of his muscles. There was a small amount of dark hair in the center of his chest that trailed down towards his navel and I followed its path with my fingers, stopping as I reached his belt. He let out a soft groan of pleasure and rolled over onto his back, pulling me with him so that I was lying on top of him. I could feel his excitement pressing against my leg, so I moved slightly so I was rubbing against him.

"Oh god, Georgia. Do you realize what you're doing?" He shifted me so that I was straddling him with my legs on either side of his hips. His hands reached behind me to unclasp my bra, letting his fingers gain access to my taut nipples. His hands cupped my breasts then slowly encircled them with caresses. Finally, he pulled me back down so our lips were pressed together, our kiss deepening as our hands continued to explore each other's body.

Just when I felt as if I was going to explode if he didn't take things further, he gently rolled to his side, carrying me with him as if we were one body. He reached down and loosened his belt and unzipped his pants, releasing his erection from its pent-up position. He then rolled over on top of me and pushed up onto his knees. My bra had fallen off as we moved, and I found myself feeling oddly free. My bare skin was exposed to his gaze and touch and I felt no inhibition in allowing it to remain that way. Whenever I had been with a man before, or with a boy to be more accurate, I had stopped myself from taking things too far. I felt too awkward and uncomfortable with the idea of being naked. But with Jon, it not only felt comfortable but strangely intoxicating.

He scooted backward on the bed so he could peel my slacks off leaving my underpants in place. His eyes took in the length of my body as his hands stroked and caressed their way over every inch of me, stopping short of the spot that was beginning to throb with increasing need. "Aren't you going to remove those?" I asked, gesturing at his pants.

He shook his head with a smile. "Not yet. There's something I need to do first." He slid back even further on the bed so that he was laying full length on his stomach with his hands grasping my hips. He pulled himself toward me, letting his tongue make a wet track up the inside of my left leg until he reached my inner thigh. He reached up with his right hand and took my left breast with a stroking, kneading motion while his tongue continued to make its way to the center of my crotch. I could tell I was wet beneath the silkiness of my panties, but the wetness intensified under the stroking of his tongue. I arched my hips against his motion, finally grasping his head in both hands in order to hold him firmly against me as my orgasm exploded in waves. I cried out in release, when he slipped his tongue under my panties to coax out the last throbs of my ebbing passion.

I lay still for a moment, luxuriating in the aftermath of the most intense physical pleasure I had ever experienced, before realizing I was the only one who had been given this pleasure. Jon was lying heavily against my legs, and I reached down to caress his head. "What about you?" I asked.

He looked up at me with a smile. "Oh, we're not finished. I just wanted you to be good and ready. It's more comfortable that way." He rolled over onto his back, stripping off his pants and underwear in one quick motion. He reached into the back pocket of his pants before tossing them aside and held up a small square foil packet.

"Is that a condom?" I peered at it with interest. "I've never seen one up close before."

He shook his head and chuckled. "You really are young, aren't you?" He gave me a mischievous look then asked, "Would you like to put it on?"

I must have looked shocked because he laughed out loud. "Don't worry. I won't put you through that your first time." He reached down and rolled it onto his penis. My eyes widened with interest as I watched him, and I realized I actually would have liked to put it on him myself.

"Can I feel it? The condom, I mean." I blushed slightly as I realized how my question must have sounded.

He looked at me with a mixture of surprise and pleasure. "By all means." He moved up so he could lie beside me again. I tentatively fingered the condom and was surprised to find it felt silky.

"Does it hurt?" I asked. "I mean it must be pretty tight."

He lay back and closed his eyes while my hand continued to run up and down the length of his condom-clad penis. "The only thing that hurts, is how badly I want to be inside you." He opened his eyes and looked at me." Take off your panties and get on top of me." I did what he said, straddling his legs again as I had before. This time, he grasped my hips and lifted me onto my feet so I was

162

positioned a few inches above his erect penis. "I'm going to lower you onto me slowly. If it hurts, or if you want to stop, just let me know." He eased me down onto him with such deliberateness I found myself wishing he would hurry up. The sensation of feeling him slide into me was more pleasant than I expected. I only felt firm warmth as he filled me more completely. "Now move up and down slowly, and tell me how you feel." I did as he asked, and tried to conjure up the words that could describe the sensations I was experiencing.

"It's nice. Not as nice as before, when your mouth was on me, but still nice."

He reached his hand up and placed a thumb on my clitoris. "We're not going for nice." He began to move his thumb to the rhythm of my hips sliding along the length of his penis. I could feel the heat building in me again, and I began to move against him more quickly. His chest was damp with sweat where my hands were placed to help keep me balanced above him. I could feel his heart pounding rapidly. My breath began to quicken as I felt my orgasm begin to build in me again, and I moaned with pleasure. Just as I felt my body release its tension in throbbing waves, I felt him cry out and buck me forcefully with his body. We both writhed in rhythm for a moment then I collapsed against his chest as if all of the strength had suddenly been wrung out of me.

We were both breathing heavily, and I lay against him in silence. When I finally sat up and looked at him, I noticed his eyes were closed and his breathing was coming in slow, regular breaths. *He's asleep!* I slowly lifted my body off his and snuggled into his side, laying one arm over his chest. The room suddenly felt chilly without the heat of our passion, so I reached down to pull the sheet up over us. I was just about to doze off when I felt the bed stir and heard the insistent purring of Ebie at my ear. "Shh, girl." I pulled her down beside me and listened contentedly to the synchronous sounds of sleep noises from the two people I loved the most. Suddenly my eyes flew open as I realized what I had just thought. *Loved? Do I love Jon?* I wasn't sure if what I felt for him at that moment was love, but it was exhilarating and delicious. For now, I was willing to let that be enough.

Chapter 25

All of us must have slept soundly for some time, because the next thing I was aware of was the sound of the phone ringing insistently. I glanced at the clock and saw it was 10 A.M. I staggered up from the bed in my sleep-addled state and shuffled my way to the kitchen. I noticed my legs felt a little wobbly, as though I had been on an extra-long walk. I smiled as I remembered the real source of my earlier exertions. I snatched the phone out of its cradle before the ringing stopped, silently reminding myself to get an answering machine in the near future.

"Hello?" I noticed my voice sounded a bit hoarse. I cleared my throat.

"Georgia? It's Thomas. I'm at the hospital and I think you'd better get down here as soon as possible."

His words caused my breath to catch. I found I couldn't make myself speak.

"Georgia? Are you still there?" His voice sounded worried and raw as if he had been awake all night. I suddenly felt guilty about my nighttime activities.

"Yes, I'm here. What's happened? Is Ida okay?" I chewed the edge of my thumb as I nervously waited for his reply.

"I'm afraid she's taken a turn for the worse. Her niece arrived a few hours ago. Ida seemed to rally for a bit. She opened her eyes and seemed to recognize Beth for a moment, but then drifted back into a coma. The doctors aren't very optimistic about her chances of recovery unless she comes out of it fairly soon." The line went silent for a moment. "They're willing to let you see her for a few minutes. Apparently, she told Beth all about you, and Beth convinced them that letting you see her might help. Sometimes hearing the voices of family and friends helps stir someone who's in her state back into consciousness. At least, they feel it's worth a try."

I nodded numbly, then realized he couldn't see me. "Of course. I'll do anything I can. Is she still in the ICU?"

"They've moved her to a private room on the critical care floor. Her vitals are stable, even though she hasn't shown much sign of improvement. It's room 4439. If you'll be coming soon, I can wait for you."

I glanced toward the bedroom door when I heard Jon stirring. "I'll need a few minutes to get ready, then I'll come right away."

"Maybe you shouldn't drive yourself. I could come get you, if you'd like."

"No!" I blurted out my response before I could stop myself. "What I mean is, I can get a ride with Jon. He stopped by again this morning, and I'm sure he won't mind driving me there." I slapped my forehead with my hand in exasperation. *Why did I just lie to him?* It wasn't that I was ashamed that Jon had stayed the night, I just wasn't ready to go public with our relationship.

The line went silent again. Finally, he spoke, "Okay then. I'll still wait here until you arrive."

After we hung up, I sat heavily at the kitchen table and covered my face with my hands. Once again, I felt my life was spiraling out of control and I was powerless to slow it down. Maybe I shouldn't have allowed myself to get so involved with Jon when I was feeling so emotional about Ida. I was beginning to second-guess my decision to sleep with him, which made me feel all the more muddled. I needed to talk to Julie, but right now I needed to get dressed and hurry to the hospital.

I walked into the bedroom and sat on the edge of the mattress. Jon looked up at me with a sleepy smile and held out his arms to me. I hesitated for a brief moment but allowed him to wrap me in his warmth. It felt so good to be close to him, I almost forgot my worries. He murmured a muffled "Good morning" against my hair and rubbed my back. Without warning, I began to cry with loud, choking sobs. His strokes stopped and his arms stiffened around me.

"What's wrong? Are you upset about last night?" His voice sounded alarmed.

I shook my head against his chest. "Thomas just called. Ida may be worse. He wants me to come to the hospital."

He pushed up from the bed, lifting me away from him so he could see my face. "Then let's go. That is, if you don't mind me coming with you." His eyes seemed to study me for a reaction.

"I was hoping you would." I lifted a corner of the sheet to wipe my face. "I'm sorry I'm such a mess. I was hoping today would bring good news. He sounded so discouraged."

He reached to kiss me gently on the forehead. "There's no need to apologize. Let's get dressed and we'll go."

On the way to the hospital, I filled Jon in on everything Thomas had told me, leaving out the part where I told him Jon had just stopped by to see me that morning. Luckily, the drive from my apartment to St. Thomas was a quick one. We were on the elevator heading to the fourth floor in less than 20 minutes. When we stepped off the elevator, we followed the signs to Ida's room. The door was closed, so I knocked quietly, before pushing it open. There was a woman sitting next to Ida's bed who I guessed to be her niece, Beth. Thomas was standing by the window, and he walked toward me as we entered.

"Georgia. I'm glad you came." His eyes moved to take in Jon. "Barnett." The two men exchanged a stiff handshake.

The woman stood and walked slowly to where we were standing. "I'm Ida's niece Beth. She's told me so much about you,

I feel as though we've already met." She surprised me by embracing me in a warm hug.

I allowed myself to return her hug then turned to look at Jon. "This is my friend, Jon Barnett." She nodded in his direction. "How is she? Thomas said she regained consciousness for a while?"

Beth nodded. "She seemed to recognize me, and for a moment I thought she was going to say something. But then she just closed her eyes and went back to sleep. The doctors did a test called an MRI, which indicated she has suffered a hemorrhagic stroke. They think it might have been caused by a hereditary problem, but they also suspect she hasn't been very careful about taking her blood pressure medication. High blood pressure is one of the main causes of this type of stroke."

I silently looked at Ida and realized I really knew so little about the person lying in front of me. She'd never given any indication she had health problems, but as I thought about it, I realized that was exactly like the Ida I did know. She always seemed to be focused on trying to help right the wrongs of life, at least when it came to preserving history. I guess that left her little time to pay attention to herself.

I walked over to the chair vacated by Beth and sat, taking Ida's hand in mine as I scooted closer to the bed. "She has been such a good friend to me. I just wish I could do something to help her now."

Beth nodded. "Why don't you sit with her? The doctors said it might help to talk to her. Sometimes that can actually bring a person back to us. The three of us will go down to the cafeteria for some coffee. Can we bring some back for you?"

I shook my head. "No thanks. I don't think I could swallow anything right now."

Her eyes misted over as she regarded me silently. "Well then, we'll be back shortly." She turned and ushered the two men out the door.

When they were gone, I moved even closer to the bed so I could study Ida carefully. Her face seemed to have aged since

I'd last seen her, but I guessed that was just the effect of her stroke and that she had been lying in the hospital bed for two days. The buns she normally wore had been loosened to allow her hair to fall to her shoulders. I was surprised at how long it was, since she usually kept it so neatly tucked. A tendril of hair had fallen across her right cheek, and I reached to push it back behind her ear, smiling as I remembered the first time I'd met her. She scared me a bit then, because she seemed so proper and in-control. I knew she would not be at all happy about being in such an out-of-control state, as she was now.

"Oh, Ida, tell me what to do. You've always been so good at giving me advice about my own silly life. Now tell me what to do about yours. I should have told you how much your help has meant to me when I had the chance. I can't bear the thought I may have missed that opportunity forever."

My mind was churning with the events of the past several days. I kept replaying the image of her walking to her door the last time I saw her. I would give anything now if I could rewind that tape and rush to her side so I could insist she tell me what she was feeling. Did she know then that something was wrong with her health? Could I have prevented the stroke from happening if I had just paid closer attention to her? I couldn't help but feel that somehow this was all, my fault. If I hadn't dragged her into the turmoil of the plans to save *The Daily Courier*, and everything else that surrounded those plans, perhaps she wouldn't have become so tired.

My thoughts were spinning out of control as I allowed my mind to fill with the possibilities. I realized this was the very time when Ida would have normally pulled me out of my misery with some insightful remark designed to help me see what I was feeling, or at least what I needed to figure out.

I wiped my eyes on the sleeve of my shirt and looked at the still figure of my friend. If I didn't know better, I could imagine she was just in a deep sleep, but she was too still. I let my fingers feel along her wrist for her pulse and was relieved to feel its steady, but faint, thump. I picked up the hand I had been holding in both of mine and lifted it to my cheek.

"I wish I could change so many things I've done. Maybe I could have kept this from happening to you. You've been such a special friend to me, but it seems all I've done from the beginning is bring trouble your way. I'm so sorry."

I let the tears flow freely without trying to stop them. I kept her hand pressed against my cheek, hoping some of my warmth could flow into her. As I held it, I voiced a silent prayer that she would recover and I would have a second chance to tell her what she meant to me. Just as I was about to place her hand back on the covers, I felt a slight movement of her hand against mine.

My eyes flew open, and I stared at her hand intently, hoping to see evidence of the movement I was certain I had felt, but it lay in my hand so heavily that I began to believe I had imagined the entire thing.

"Ida? Can you hear me? Can you open your eyes?"

Her eyes remained closed, but once again I could feel the slight movement of her hand. At the same time, I became aware that Jon, Beth, and Thomas had returned and were standing next to me. I looked at them and pointed at Ida, never letting go of her hand.

"Her hand moved. It wasn't exactly a squeeze, but I could definitely feel a slight pressure. Twice."

Beth moved closer to the bed and put her hand on Ida's leg. "Aunt Ida? Can you hear me? It's Beth. If you can hear me open your eyes." We all stared intently at her hoping for a sign that she was coming around, but her eyes remained closed and her hand remained limp in mine. Thomas had bolted for the nurse's station when he heard what I said. One of the floor nurses rushed in with Thomas close on her heels. The nurse walked swiftly to check her monitor and listen to her chest with a stethoscope. She then moved to her feet and ran a metal object up her instep, then lifted one arm and released it. We watched her expectantly, but she turned to us with a grim look and a slight headshake.

"I'm sorry. There's no indication that she's regaining consciousness."

"But her hand moved! Twice." I looked up at the nurse desperately.

"Medical studies seem to suggest that we can hear what is being said to us even from a comatose state. So, it's possible she was responding to your voice or to what you were saying to her."

"Does it mean she will get better?" I looked at her hopefully.

She seemed to hesitate before speaking, as if she wanted to choose her words carefully. "Sometimes that happens. But in this case, there's no indication she is improving. Her vital signs are weak, and she is physically unresponsive. People who suffer the kind of stroke she did usually decline rapidly, though they occasionally rally for a brief time before returning to the comatose state." She looked at each of us sympathetically. "I'll ask the doctor to come in to speak to you when he's free. For now, the best thing you can do for her is to let her know you're here by your touch and by talking to her." She placed a hand on Ida's shoulder for a second before turning to leave the room.

I stood stiffly and moved away from the bed. My brain felt numb, but at the same time, my body seemed to tingle with unspent energy. I was vaguely aware of Jon thanking the nurse in murmured tones, and I felt grateful he was there. Yet, I had the urge to run from the room and everything that had happened over the past several days.

Beth came to stand beside me and placed a hand on my shoulder. "Why don't you take a break? Go outside with Jon and get some fresh air. I promise to send Thomas to find you if there is any change."

I nodded at them glumly. "I won't be long. I just need to move a little bit."

Jon took my hand and led me to the door. Before we left, I turned back to gaze once more at Ida. She seemed the same as when I had first entered the hospital room, but I knew in my heart she had tried to communicate with me. How ironic, even near death she was still trying to help me. I only wished I could do the same for her.

Chapter 26

For four more days, Ida remained in the same state as I had left her. I returned to her bedside frequently, and each time I watched intently for any indication that she was aware of my presence. The doctor explained she had suffered the stroke because of a leaky blood vessel, due to what was known as an AV malformation. Apparently, the walls of the vessel become stretched and thin over time, as a result of frequent increases in blood pressure, causing them to eventually leak. This defect was described as rare, but Ida must have been aware of it because her medical record indicated she was on high doses of medicine to control her blood pressure. The doctor kept emphasizing there was very little that could have been done to prevent a stroke from occurring, short of surgery to try to repair the damage. Beth later told me her aunt had been aware for years of the surgery option, but decided against it.

I kept trying to talk to her, as the nurse suggested, but I never again felt even the slightest indication she was aware of me or of what I was saying. Most of the time, I just rattled away about the weather, and what was going on around the hospital. But whenever I found myself alone with her, I spoke more intimately.

173

I told her about the recent development in my relationship with Jon, and how I was confused by what it meant. I didn't really have any experience that could help me sort out the differences between love and lust, and I was struggling to make sense of my feelings.

I hadn't had time to talk to Julie much about any of it. I had given her a call after my first visit to the hospital to let her know about Ida. Since then, our conversations had been limited to the couple of times she came by the hospital to drag me downstairs for a cup of coffee. During one of those visits, she looked at me curiously when Jon kept putting a possessive arm around me whenever Thomas entered the room. When we finally had a few minutes alone she asked me pointedly if something was going on. I tried to give her the "Reader's Digest" version of what transpired between us, and about the odd feeling I had that Ida wanted me to go out with Thomas. I had to admit, Thomas seemed to have more than just a professional interest in me, but I mostly chalked it up to the odd circumstances we had been thrown into. Spending so much time at the hospital with him, as well as Jon and Beth, allowed me to realize emphatically that my feelings for him were strictly platonic. My respect for him had been growing exponentially. I could see us becoming good friends, but that was as far as it went. With Jon, on the other hand, the passion we shared deepened with each passing day. It became joined by another feeling I could only imagine was what being in love felt like.

Jon stuck by me since we got the call from Thomas to come to the hospital. He left, every now and then, to shower and change into fresh clothes in his hotel room, or look in on Ebie to make sure she had food and water. Other than that, he was pretty much constantly with me. We didn't say much to each other while we were at the hospital. It was like we didn't need to. There was a silent communication that seemed to flow between us, where he was able to read my thoughts and act on them without me having to explain what I was thinking. It was odd, really, given the confusing and unclear nature of our relationship since we the first time we met. It was almost as if bonding with him physically had created a mental and emotional link between us, as well. Whatever it was, I was grateful for the change. It felt good to lean on his strength, knowing that whatever happened, he would be there to help me through it.

Our physical connection had been continuing to grow as well, even though there were nights when the only thing we had the energy for was to collapse on the bed in exhaustion and fall asleep wrapped in each other's arms. Not that we hadn't made love again since our first time. Oh yes, we had certainly done that. While it may not have had the same level of excitement as our first time, it was every bit as intense and even more passionate as we grew more comfortable with each other.

Thomas and Beth had been spending countless hours at the hospital, as well. The four of us began to look more than a little ragged around the edges as the hours slipped away without any signs of change from Ida. Shortly after I first visited her at the hospital, a medical resident placed a breathing device on her face, and a nurse fitted her with a catheter. They explained these were necessary steps to help buy her a little more time to see if she could pull out of the coma on her own.

The attending physician, Dr. Frazier, came by at the end of his rounds on the sixth day after her stroke. He brought a small entourage of medical staff and residents with him who all peered at her chart and checked the various machines that beeped their report of her condition and dripped fluids into her veins. After several minutes of discussion among themselves, Dr. Frazier turned to look at the four of us.

"There's a small conference room just past the nurse's station. Why don't we go there so we can talk?" He left the room without waiting for our reply, followed closely by the other medical attendees. The four of us looked at each other wordlessly, then turned to follow them. Once we were all seated in the conference room, Dr. Frazier leaned on the table and looked at Beth.

"I'm afraid there's nothing more we can do for your aunt. Her urine output indicates her kidneys are shutting down, and her heart rate is growing weaker. Frankly, the only thing keeping her alive at this point is the respirator." He paused to allow his words to sink in before continuing. "We feel it would be the best thing for her to allow her to go peacefully. We can give her something to relax her as she goes through the process so she will not be in any pain."

Beth stood and stared wide-eyed at the doctor. "You're saying to just let her die?"

Dr. Frazier looked at her kindly. "I know how hard it must be to consider that allowing her to pass on may be the best thing we can do for her. I can assure you, if there was even the slightest indication she could recover, we would never make that suggestion."

Beth sat heavily in her chair, covering her face with her hands. Jon had grasped my hand tightly when the doctor began to speak. He released it now to wrap his arm around me and draw me nearer to him. Thomas removed his glasses and wiped his eyes with a handkerchief, then cleared his throat.

"If you remove the respirator, is there a chance she will continue to breathe on her own?" he asked.

Dr. Frazier shook his head. "I've seen it occur in rare cases, but I don't anticipate that happening here. She's been comatose too long, and there have been absolutely no signs of improvement."

Thomas looked at Beth, then at me. "I don't believe she would want to live this way—hooked up to a machine forcing her to breathe artificially."

I nodded silently and looked at Beth. As the only true family member in the room, the call would have to be hers. "Beth? Would you like a little time to think this over? Maybe there's someone you should call?" I asked.

She nodded glumly. "My parents. They've never been that close to Aunt Ida, at least not for several years. But I think it's only fair I discuss this with them. I want to call my husband, too. He would be here with me except he had an important meeting at his job that he needed to stay in town for. We decided I would come on ahead of him and let him know how things seemed. He'll want to come as soon as possible now."

Dr. Frazier stood and began to move toward the door. "We can talk again in the morning. I suggest you phone your family right away so they can get here as quickly as possible. If you decide to go forward with our suggestion, we can make the arrangements as soon as you're ready." He left the room with the troop of medical personnel on his heels.

The four of us sat in silence, each lost in our own thoughts of what had to be decided. Thomas was the first to speak. "Would you like me to call anyone for you Beth? I know they don't know me, but perhaps it would be easier if I made the call."

Beth shook her head. "Thanks, but I think it's better if I phone them. I just need a little more time to wrap my head around this, then I'll go use the pay phone in the waiting room."

Beth had been sleeping on a foldout cot in Ida's room since she had arrived in Nashville. The arrangement didn't allow much comfort, and it certainly didn't provide any semblance of privacy. "Why don't you use the phone at my apartment?" I asked. "It's not far from here. Jon can take you there, if you'd like, and you can rest a while and freshen up." I looked at him inquisitively and he nodded.

"Thanks. Perhaps it would be better to talk somewhere private." She rose wearily and looked at Jon. "Would you mind if I spent a few moments with my aunt first? I can meet you in the lobby in about ten minutes."

"Take all the time you need. I'll pull the car around and wait for you by the door to Admissions and Registration."

The rest of us looked at one another before wordlessly moving toward the door. We were four acquaintances who, through the power of shared grief, had become—if not friends— at least friendly. There were a lot of sniffing sounds and cleared throats as we left the room. Beth headed down the hallway, followed by Thomas, who said he was going to phone his office to let them know what was happening. It suddenly dawned on me that all of our plans for the new journalism program had been put on hold in the wake of Ida's illness. I wondered if that was going to cause any permanent damage to the process. As if he read my mind, Jon took my hand in his again.

"Don't worry about the *Courier*. I talked to the Belmont administration yesterday and things are moving ahead as planned. I've asked one of our board members to fly down to oversee things, to make sure there are no hold-ups. He'll be arriving sometime today. "

I smiled at him gratefully. "I'm embarrassed to say I haven't given it much thought until now. Ida would be devastated if we allowed her situation to prevent us from seeing this through."

He nodded thoughtfully. "She was a tough old bird. Sorry, I don't mean any disrespect by that comment. It's just how I thought of her, and not in an unkind way. I always admired her toughness. Seeing her lying in that bed day after day hasn't been easy to accept."

I took both his hands in mine. "What do you think Beth will decide?"

He shrugged. "She doesn't seem to have much choice. It's a tough call to make, but like the doctor said, there hasn't been any indication Ida will get any better. I certainly wouldn't want to be forced to live hooked-up to all of those machines. It's not really living, is it?"

"I suppose not. Although, if she really can hear what is said to her, then she's in some halfway place between life and death."

We left the conference room together. Jon kissed me on the forehead then went to retrieve his car. He had been so incredibly understanding throughout this whole ordeal. He never pushed me to talk about how I felt about our relationship, nor asked me to answer the questions he posed to me during what now seemed like such a long time ago. For once, I didn't mind his reticence. It was a relief not to have to analyze what was going on. My brain already felt like it was dealing with as much as it could possibly handle.

I made my way down the hall toward Ida's room. Thomas was standing in the hallway talking to a nurse who I recognized as his friend from the ER. Although I had only spoken to her briefly, she had become a familiar sight in our ranks, because she had been popping into Ida's room off and on every day since her admission. I nodded at them and walked to her door, pausing to look inside before entering, in case Beth was still with her. The room was empty except for the steady sounds from the machines. I walked in and closed the door behind me, pulling a chair close to the bed so I could take her hand. I couldn't see any change in her face. She still looked as if she was just sleeping, although the rise and fall of her chest in rhythm with the respirator made it impossible to ignore her actual state.

I took a deep breath and prepared to talk to my friend. It was time for me to say what I needed to tell her; to let her know how I felt about her and how much she meant to me. I realized it might be the last time I ever had the chance to say those things to her and I didn't want to leave anything unsaid.

Chapter 27

The funeral service took place three days later. Ida's sister and her husband arrived the day after Dr. Frazier spoke with us, and Beth's husband came that same afternoon. That night, we all gathered at her bedside to witness the removal of her respirator in silent hope she would respond by breathing on her own. But it was not to be. At least, her passing appeared to be peaceful. She made a slight gurgling sound when the tube was withdrawn from her throat, then her chest seemed to deflate as her last breath left her body. The only other sounds in the room were the quiet sobs from those of us present as we held one another or reached to grasp her hand or stroke her head.

I never thought of Ida as particularly religious since, to my knowledge, she never attended church services. But apparently, her Will indicated she wished to be buried according to the traditions of the Baptist church. That meant her body was laid out for what was called "viewing and visitation" at Woodlawn Funeral Home for a full day before the actual burial service took place. I attended both, though I did my best to stay well back from the sight of her laid out for viewing. I just couldn't bring myself to look at her lying in the cold casket, surrounded by flowers and photos from her past. In retrospect, I suppose it wouldn't have been much different than seeing her lying comatose in a hospital bed. The difference for me was, whereas the latter held the hope of awakening and continued life, the former just meant she was gone. I knew some people regarded death as a continuation of existence, with the promise of heaven or rebirth—life after life, as it was sometimes called. I wanted to believe that some part of each of us continued after our body stopped functioning, I had only experienced death as a final curtain that closed over the existence of a person I had known. The thought that I would never be able to see Ida again, or hear her words of guidance and support, absolutely crushed me.

I barely left my apartment during the days following her funeral. Thomas kindly told me to wait until the following Monday to start my work at the University, and I accepted his offer with relief. It was two weeks later than we originally agreed upon, but a lot of things had happened in that short time. I couldn't imagine being able to focus on anything that would require as much attention as a new job. Especially since starting that job, and spending my days on the Belmont campus, would be so infused with the memory of Ida's involvement in our mutual project; the project I still believed was a contributor, if not an outright cause, of her illness and death.

Jon remained in Nashville until the internment service, before returning to D.C. to wrap up some final details on the relocation of *The Daily Courier*. Truthfully, I didn't mind him leaving. I felt the need to wallow in my grief and misery. That was a lot easier to do if there wasn't anyone around to have to apologize to or explain how I was feeling. I remained in my apartment alone, moving from the sofa to the kitchen to the bed, rarely staying more than a short time in any one place. I could barely sleep, and eating was out of the question, since my throat seemed to have lost the ability to function.

Julie had been phoning daily, as had Jon, but most of the time I just let the phone ring unanswered. I was glad I hadn't gotten around to purchasing that answering machine so I wouldn't have to listen to their complaints about my silence. I spoke to my parents once. They phoned to tell me they heard I had been fired from *The Nashville News*, and began to launch into their usual diatribe of scolding and criticism. After learning about Ida's death, they had grown uncharacteristically quiet. I couldn't really call their response supportive; that would have called for them to step too far outside of their comfort zone. But I guess even they were not immune to noticing the precarious emotional perch I was teetering on. Even Ebie seemed disturbed by my behavior. She followed me from room to room, mewing quietly, and leaping onto my lap whenever I managed to sit still for a few minutes.

On the third day of my self-imposed isolation, exhaustion must have finally caught up with me, because I found myself being awakened from a restless, dream-filled sleep, by a loud pounding on my door. At first, I thought I was still dreaming, but I heard Julie yelling that if I didn't open up, she was going to have the fire department break the door down. I shuffled over to the door and pulled it open.

"Why haven't you been answering your phone? Jon and Thomas have been ringing mine off the hook, asking me if I've heard from you. Apparently, you haven't been answering their calls either." She paused her ranting long enough to take a close look at me. "My god, girl, you look terrible!"

"Thanks." I turned away from her and returned to the sofa, sinking into the blanket I crawled out of when she awakened me.

Julie stood for a moment, her eyes taking in the messy state of my apartment and my disheveled, unwashed appearance, before striding purposefully toward me. "The first thing I'm going to do is run a bath for you. The second is to find you something to eat."

I looked up at her petulantly. "Is this what they call 'tough love'? Because if it is, you needn't bother."

She blinked at me before turning to walk in the direction of my bathroom. A few seconds later I heard the sound of water running, followed by the opening and closing of cabinet doors.

I pulled the blanket over my head in hopes of drowning out the sounds of her activity and dissuading her from continuing her pursuit of my return to life. No sooner had I begun to slip off the edge of consciousness into sleep, I felt the blanket being yanked off me. I opened my eyes halfway and saw her standing before me with a mug of something steamy that smelled surprisingly good.

"Sit up and drink this. It's tomato soup. You didn't have much to choose from in your kitchen, but this should do for now."

I took the mug from her, wrapping my hands around its welcoming warmth and letting the aroma fill my nostrils. "It smells good." I took a small sip and allowed a small moan to escape my lips. "Tastes good, too."

"How long has it been since you've eaten anything?"

"I don't remember."

She shook her head and turned to walk into the bathroom, returning a minute later.

"I've filled the tub with warm water. Why don't you slip into it before it gets cold?" She took the mug from my hand. "I'll warm this up and bring it to you once you're settled."

I handed over my mug and allowed her to help me to my feet. I shuffled into the bathroom, discarding my clothes as I walked. The tub was filled about three-quarters and gave off the aroma of something flowery. I slowly eased my body down into the water. The temperature felt just right. It wasn't so hot that it burned my skin, but it was warm enough that I could feel my muscles begin to soften as I settled down into its depths. Ebie hopped up onto the toilet seat and viewed me curiously. I guess I must have looked content, because she walked to the edge and carefully dipped one paw into the water before lifting it back out quickly.

I laughed at her as I flicked a few drops of water in her direction. "You know you don't like to get wet. Just sit there and keep me company."

Julie walked in carrying my mug of soup and handed it to me, then lifted Ebie onto her lap so she could take her place on the toilet seat. I took a sip of the soup then smiled at her. "I hate to admit it, but this is just what I needed."

She seemed pleased, although the grim set to her mouth had still not completely relaxed. "I'm glad to hear it. You know, you really had me worried. I wasn't sure what state I was going to find you in." She stroked Ebie's back thoughtfully. "My god, Georgia, you could have died in here and no one would have known."

I frowned at her as I considered what she said. Tears began to form in the corners of my eyes, and I let them drip slowly down my cheeks. "I'm not sure if that would have been such a bad thing. The pain I've been feeling since Ida died has been almost unbearable. I keep wishing I could make it stop."

She dipped her head and laid her cheek against Ebie's soft fur. When she raised it again, I could see tears glistening on her face. "I know this has been hard for you. You got really close to her in a short period of time. But I have to wonder if there's something more going on."

My eyes opened wider in surprise and I felt something grab at my chest. "What do you mean?"

She seemed to weigh her thoughts before answering. "I just meant that maybe your pain is not just about the loss of Ida, but it may also be because you're afraid."

I set the mug down and sunk a little deeper into the water. The water was beginning to cool a bit, but I wasn't ready to get out of the tub yet. "What could I possibly be afraid of?" I barely recognized my voice as I spoke. It sounded faint and tinged with something that sounded like regret.

"Well, let's see. I could come up with any number of things off the top of my head. You lost the first job you ever had, which surely must have made you feel like the rug had been pulled out from under your feet. Your relationship with Jon has heated up, and although you still haven't given me details about that, I imagine it has been quite an earth-moving turn of events. You're about to start a new job you really know very little about, which for someone who likes to plan everything out to the most minute detail, must be quite anxiety provoking. Then, to top it all off, you've lost someone who became very important in your life very quickly. Someone who seemed to give you a sense of security in her guidance and support. Pick any one of those things, and I think you can make a case for a good-old fear-based depression. "

I blinked at her as I considered her speculation. There was nothing she said that I could deny. Yet, admitting to myself that fear was the main source of my misery was uncomfortable. I knew courage was something that had evaded me through most of my childhood. Even now, I had to push myself to try anything even remotely new, but I believed I had gotten braver about venturing out into unknown territory since starting work at *The Nashville News*. Nonetheless, stability and consistency made me feel secure, and those things had been far too absent in my life in the past few months. "I don't know, Julie. Maybe you're right. All I know is, I feel worse than I ever have in my entire life." Something occurred to me. "You know that therapist you mentioned seeing? Do you think you could get me an appointment to talk with him?"

Julie nodded. "It's a woman. But, yes, I'm sure that can be arranged. She's really nice, and she's helped me a lot."

I began to struggle up from the tub. My legs felt wobbly, and I had to use my arms to push myself up using the edge for support. Julie grabbed my robe from the back of the bathroom door, wrapping it around me as she helped me step out onto the floor.

I looked at her gratefully. "You're always here for me, aren't you? I don't know how, but you always seem to know what to say to bring me out of whatever place I've gotten myself stuck into."

She snorted out a laugh. "When you let me, you mean. You're not the easiest person to reach sometimes. Must be that stubborn Irish streak."

I was glad for the lightness she intentionally injected into the moment. The worry and grief I had wrapped myself in for the last few days had been weighing on me heavily. I welcomed the relief that came from feeling it lessen even a tiny bit. I still didn't understand why I let everything bother me so much, but at least I now had a plan that might help me figure some of it out.

That was all Julie's doing. She'd stuck by me through thick and thin, and never wavered in her loving support. But she wasn't a pushover, and she didn't let me get away with much self-deceit or denial. I guess that friendship, when it helps you be your best self while gently pointing out your worst, was a priceless gift. A troublesome gift at times, to be sure, and one that came with some pretty hefty responsibilities. But I was growing to realize it was a gift worth whatever challenges it came with.

Chapter 28

The following Monday, which also happened to coincide with the first day of April, I found myself walking through the door to the Belmont College Communications Department with a spring in my step. Despite the day being known as *April Fool's Day*, I had a good feeling about what was about to take place. In the days that followed Julie's tough love intervention in my apartment, I had grown steadily stronger, mostly due to the continued ministrations of her daily visits, which usually involved bags of food and mandatory walks around the neighborhood. By Sunday night, I was actually looking forward to the start of my new career with only a faint overshadowing of anxiety.

Thomas was hard at work digging through his usual stack of papers when I arrived. His head snapped up when I knocked quietly on the doorframe, and he rushed around his desk to clasp my hand firmly in his.

"Welcome, welcome! Why don't you hang your coat over there and I'll show you to your desk?" He gestured to an empty chair to his right that was only partially covered with books. I draped my coat over the back of the chair and placed my satchel on the floor beside it. When I turned around, I found him shoving

187

aside an assorted accumulation of books and papers that mostly obliterated the top of a small wooden desk.

"I'm afraid you'll have to work in here until we can make other arrangements."

I looked around the crowded office and smiled. "It reminds me of the newsroom at *The News*. I used to think of it as organized chaos."

His sudden laugh filled the room, and I was reminded of the last time I was in his office. He laughed in much the same way on that occasion, when I asked if I should call him "Boss". Ida had been with us. In fact, it was the last day I saw her before I was called to the hospital.

Thomas must have noticed my sudden change of mood because he placed a hand on my shoulder before quickly removing it again. "I miss her, too. I hope working here won't be too uncomfortable for you. "

I smiled at him in what I hoped was a reassuring way. "Not at all. It will be good to be busy with something useful. I'm afraid I've been wallowing in my own misery for far too long. I need to occupy my mind with something besides myself."

He nodded and stood with his hands in his pockets. "Just promise you'll let me know if it all gets to be too much, too soon. I have a tendency to get wrapped up in my work, to the extent that I become oblivious of anything else."

I was grateful for his honesty, that I could be straightforward with him about my feelings. "Thank you. Now, tell me what you want me to do."

He clapped his hands together and laughed in delight. I was going to have to get used to his sudden bursts of merriment, since it seemed to be a common characteristic of his. It wasn't unpleasant. In fact, it was a relief to be around someone who wasn't always cloaked in mystery. A sudden image of Jon came to my mind, and I shook my head to banish it. He still hadn't returned from D.C. Even though I longed to see him again, I was more than a little nervous about his return. I felt we had come a long way since our first fateful meeting at the Ball, and I felt closer to him than I ever imagined I could. But there were still a lot of unanswered questions hanging between us.

Thomas ran his hands through his hair and gestured at the stacks of papers and books scattered throughout the room. "I'm afraid your first assignment won't be that exciting. I need you to try to put this mess into some sort of order. It's gotten so bad, even I can't find what I need. There are some bookshelves over there and a row of filing cabinets. Once things are cleared off them, you should have enough space to store most of this stuff. Just let my secretary know if you need anything else." He glanced at his watch walking quickly to his desk, snatching up a briefcase and a stack of papers before striding toward the door. "Well, I'm off to class. I'll be back in a couple of hours, but, as I said, just let Mrs. Stayhill know if you need anything."

After he left, I stood for a few minutes surveying the contents of the room. The energy I arrived with seemed to have left me, and I found myself wishing I could return to the comfort of my apartment. Just when I was about to talk myself into doing just that, I heard a voice behind me. I turned to find Mrs. Stayhill standing just inside the door. I met her briefly when Thomas offered me the assistant job. She was a smartly dressed woman whom I guessed to be in her mid-50s. Her hair was neatly piled into what was known as a bouffant hairstyle which was a bit of a throwback to the late 60s when it was known as the "Jackie Kennedy" style. In fact, she looked a little like Mrs. Kennedy with her sleek dark hair that sported just a few streaks of silver, and a perfectly tailored two-piece suit. She was also soft-spoken, as Mrs. Kennedy had been, which gave the impression of calm assurance.

"I'm sorry if I startled you. I just wanted to welcome you on your first day here. Professor Bookman asked me to look in on you to see if you have everything you need."

I smiled at her appreciatively. "Thank you, but I'm not sure anything could help put this place in order, short of a bulldozer."

She smiled her understanding as her eyes scanned the room. "I'm afraid organization is not one of Professor Bookman's better traits. We tend to forgive him for that, because he has so many other redeeming qualities. Might I suggest a cup of coffee to start with? Or perhaps you prefer tea?"

The idea of something, anything, with caffeine suddenly sounded extremely appealing. "Coffee would be great."

She turned and gestured for me to follow. "Let's have it in the break room. There's a little more space to sit in there."

I followed her down the hall to a room at the front of the building. It was a small area, only about half the size of Thomas' office, but it felt spacious in the absence of clutter. There were windows looking out over the Belmont campus, allowing sunlight to spill across a counter containing a sink, coffee maker, and several cups. An ancient looking refrigerator stood next to the counter, and a table and six chairs filled the center of the room.

She filled two mugs with rich-looking coffee and placed them on the table, along with a small container of milk. "There's sugar in that bowl, if you use it." She turned back to the counter to grab napkins and spoons before taking a seat across from me. "Sometimes we have donuts or cookies one of the students brings in, but I'm afraid the cupboard is bare this morning."

I took a sip of coffee and decided to add a little milk to the strong brew. "Coffee is fine. I had breakfast before I left home."

The truth was, I hadn't had anything but a glass of water and a slice of toast before leaving my apartment. My pre-work jitters kept me from being able to stomach anything else. I took another hearty sip settling back in the chair. I could feel the warmth of the beverage seeping into my body and the caffeine was beginning to give my brain a needed jolt. I looked across at Mrs. Stayhill to find her eyeing me politely.

"I'm sorry for the loss of your friend. I didn't know her well, but she seemed like a fine person."

The mention of Ida had new tears welling in my eyes. I hastily dabbed at them with my napkin while nodding at her comment. "She was. I've been missing her a lot."

She surprised me by reaching across the table to pat my hand. "When I lost my mother, someone told me 'the end is just the beginning of an even longer story'. I had no idea what that meant at the time, but now I realize that when someone passes from this life, they leave behind a trail of memories and impressions that, over time, form themselves into a story we carry with us. I suspect it will be that way for you as you revisit the times you've shared with your friend."

Her insight surprised me. No one else had said anything about Ida's death that even remotely suggested something good could be gained from it. I liked the idea of her memory becoming part of a story I could create and add to as time went by. "That's helpful. Thank you for sharing it with me."

She smiled warmly as she placed her mug on the table and folded her hands on her lap. "Now. Let's talk about what you need to tackle your first assignment. We have a supply closet down the hall with an assortment of file folders and storage devices that might be useful. Would you like to see it?"

"I guess there's no time like the present, as they say."

"Yes, indeed. Let's go see what we can find."

We carried our coffee items to the sink to wash and place in the draining rack. I followed Mrs. Stayhill down the hall in the direction of Thomas' office, stopping along the way in front of double doors. The supply closet turned out to be just an overstuffed set of shelves recessed into the wall, but at least it appeared to contain items that could be helpful with the chore I was facing.

"This will be fine. I think I'll start organizing the piles into different piles, then I'll take a closer look at what's in here." I turned to smile at her. "Thank you for the coffee and the advice. I appreciate both of them."

She ducked her head in embarrassment lifting a hand to wave off my thanks. "Just remember, I'm right next door if you need anything. It can get pretty noisy in here when the students come around, but at other times, it's entirely too quiet for my taste. It will be nice to have someone to talk to from time to time."

As she left, I thought back to what she said about every ending being a beginning. I wondered what this new start to my professional life would hold in store for me. I began to feel my previous anxiety slipping away, to be replaced by something that felt oddly like anticipation. It was a good feeling, and I found myself smiling as I turned to walk back in the direction of Thomas' office. Even the organized chaos I was about to face didn't seem so daunting anymore.

Chapter 29

When Thomas returned three hours later, I had made quite a stab at shifting things around enough to begin to see how they could possibly be put into some sort of order. I unearthed a radio from the clutter, and found a station that filled the room with the lively sounds of top-40 music broadcast from a location in the downtown area. The music did a lot to cut through the library-like quiet of the room and I found myself moving in rhythm to the tunes. One of my first jobs had been to clear off the bookshelves. I had just started to refill them with books when Thomas walked in.

"Wow! You've been busy! Oh, where did you find my old radio? I've been looking for that thing for months."

I laughed. "It was under a stack of papers over there." I pointed to a now empty corner of the room. "I hope you don't mind that I turned it on."

He shook his head and began to shuffle to the beat of the music. "Not at all, although you might have to put up with my off-key singing and uncoordinated dance steps when the spirit moves me."

I watched him unsuccessfully attempt to match the rhythm of the song playing. "I can live with that. How did your classes go?"

He stopped attempting to dance and walked over to drop his briefcase on his desk. "Good. I have a great group of students this semester. They're all eagerness and enthusiasm. It's kind of like lecturing to a bunch of puppies."

I laughed at the image this brought to my mind. "I hope they don't have some of the bad habits that puppies have."

His laugh joined mine, and soon we were spouting out descriptions of how puppies might behave in a classroom. Our laughter must have become quite loud because I suddenly became aware of Mrs. Stayhill standing at the door blinking at us curiously. Thomas noticed her, too, and tried to stifle his laughter.

"Hello, Mrs. Stayhill. Georgia and I were just imagining what it would be like if students were puppies. What a mess that would be!"

She shook her head in disapproval, though I could see she was barely containing her own urge to laugh. "I see. Did you remember your lunch engagement with the Provost?"

Thomas swallowed his laughter and ran his hand through his hair. "I'm glad you reminded me." He glanced at his watch with a sigh. "I guess I'd better get moving. It wouldn't do for me to keep him waiting. Especially since I'm hoping to convince him that relocating *The Daily Courier* here deserves more space than they've currently allocated for the project." He looked over at me curiously. "Georgia, why don't you come with me? The old buzzard is known for having an appreciative eye for pretty women. Your presence just might help persuade him."

I looked back and forth from Thomas to Mrs. Stayhill to see if he was joking and to gauge her reaction to his suggestion. "That's an excellent idea, Professor. It will give Georgia a chance to learn a little about how things work around here."

Thomas clapped his hands together. "Okay then. That's settled. I'll just need a few moments and I'll be ready to leave."

Mrs. Stayhill looked at me reassuringly. "He's right about the Provost, but don't worry. He's relatively harmless. Just smile at him and listen carefully to everything he says. It might help our cause, and you could even learn some things in the process."

"Okay. If you think it's a good idea. I just wasn't prepared to meet someone in such an important position on my first day here."

She gave a little flutter of her fingers. "You needn't be intimidated by Provost Crawford. I've known him since he was an assistant professor. He had quite a reputation as a ladies' man when he first came here, but the truth is, he's totally devoted to his wife and two children. He just likes to hang on to the image. Makes him feel virile, I imagine."

I was a little surprised by her forthright comment. Apparently, Mrs. Stayhill was not as prim and proper as her appearance suggested. I was reminded once again not to jump to conclusions about a person based strictly upon first impressions.

"That's an interesting image you've just painted of him. I'll keep it in mind when we meet." I began to gather my things so I would be ready when Thomas returned.

"The best advice I can give you is what I said earlier; listen and learn. You'd be surprised how much you can learn about a person if you pay attention to not only what they say, but how they say it."

The dining room, where we were to meet the Provost, was located on the opposite side of the Belmont Mansion from Fidelity Hall, the site of Thomas' office, and now mine. It was on the first floor of Founder's Hall, which also housed offices of the Provost and other administrators.

The room was bustling with activity when we arrived. Thomas made his way to a private dining area to the left of the main hall, which was quieter and contained only half a dozen tables. The tables were mostly occupied by men in suits, which caused me to feel more than a little conspicuous, not only for the minority of my gender, but also for the informality of my dress. Thomas must have noticed my hesitation because he placed a hand firmly against my back and guided me toward a table that was empty except for a somewhat portly man, with salt-and-pepper hair, who was tapping his fingers impatiently against his water glass. He stood abruptly when he noticed us and thrust his hand in Thomas' direction.

"Bookman. Good to see you again." His gaze turned to me with a lift of his eyebrows. "Who is this lovely creature?" He was staring at me as if I was the main course of a meal that he couldn't wait to start. I had to keep myself from giggling at the sudden image of a salivating fox that came to mind.

Thomas looked at me with a firm set to his mouth and a slight shake of his head as if he had read my mind. "This is my new assistant, Georgia Ayres. She's been a key player in the plans to relocate *The Daily Courier* here and expand the journalism program."

The provost's eyes narrowed at Thomas' introduction. "I see. She barely looks old enough to be out of high school." Again, the image of a fox, albeit a paunchy balding fox, filled my mind.

Thomas shuffled the coins in his pockets nervously as he looked from the Provost to me. I couldn't guess his thoughts, but I imagined he was wondering if bringing me along was such a good idea after all. Mrs. Stayhill's advice suddenly came to me so I reached out my hand toward the Provost with uncharacteristic boldness.

"It's a pleasure to meet you, Provost Crawford. Mrs. Stayhill has been telling me all about you."

He seemed to shrink at the mention of her name, and his previous bluster disappeared.

"That so. I imagine she had a few choice words to say about me. Did she tell you we used to date when I first came here? You know what they say about a woman scorned, and all that. No, I doubt she painted me in a very flattering light."

His comment shocked me. The idea that Mrs. Stayhill and the Provost had once dated was a huge surprise, and one I couldn't picture. It was as peculiar as imagining that Jackie Kennedy would have gone out with Richard Nixon. It was just unfathomable!

Luckily, Thomas saved me from having to respond to his news by suggesting we take our seats. He held a chair out for me, then sat in the one to my right, which conveniently placed the Provost on his other side, and to my relief, as far away from me as possible. The Provost cleared his throat and glanced around the room, nodding in the direction of two men who were finishing their lunch at an adjacent table. He leaned toward Thomas to speak.

"That man with President Ralston has more money than he knows what to do with. Hopefully, Ralston is convincing him to throw some of it our way." He chuckled and leaned back in his chair.

Thomas glanced at the two men and nodded. "I'm glad to hear you use the word 'our'. I assume that means you're fully onboard with our plans?"

The Provost sat up straighter in his chair and cleared his throat. "I have to admit, I wasn't keen on it at first. I've come around to seeing that the idea has merit. It could be just what the College needs to draw the attention of some pretty powerful people, and I'm not just talking about in Nashville. A move relocating a well-known newspaper onto a college campus and developing a curriculum around its publication, I don't believe that's ever been done before." He appeared to become lost in thought for a moment. "No, I don't think there's ever been a precedent set for this kind of a venture. Puts Belmont in pioneer territory, and not in a bad way."

Thomas looked at me out of the corner of his eyes and I could see a gleam of excitement in them. "That makes what I want to talk to you about a little easier. We're going to need more space on campus in order to make this work. The existing rooms allocated for the journalism program are barely enough to provide office and teaching space for our faculty. The money Mrs. Hood donated to add a new wing onto Fidelity Hall should be enough to allow us to expand those services. But bringing a newspaper production here will require designated space of a different sort."

The Provost leaned back in his chair. "What do you have in mind?"

"Freeman Hall. There's more than enough room on the main floor for us to set up the equipment and staffing space we'll need to publish *The Daily Courier*. We wouldn't need to interfere with the offices upstairs. We'd just take over the downstairs area."

Provost Crawford snickered and leaned forward so he could speak without being overheard. "I'm sure President Ralston will be glad to hear you don't intend to put him out of his office." He leaned back again and took a long drink of the iced tea the waitress placed in front of him. "I'll have to give your suggestion some thought, but it just might work. That is, assuming the President agrees to both give up that space, and provide the funding for its renovation." He suddenly looked at me as though he just remembered I was present. "What do you think, young lady? Will this plan of your boss's work, or will it end up being my worst nightmare?"

I had been sipping a coke, then placed it on the table, considering Thomas' suggestion. Freeman Hall was located just behind the Mansion. I read a little about the history of the building during one of my visits to Ida and had been impressed with its historical significance. I remembered it had originally been called North Front, since it sat on a hill at the north end of the campus, overlooking downtown Nashville. In the past, it housed a notable array of services, including a dormitory, dining room, classrooms, reception areas, and an assembly hall. It had even been the site of Nashville's first radio station back in the early 1920s, which meant it must have been set-up with some fairly decent wiring and soundproofing. At the present time, it housed the office of the President, and several other College administrators, on the upper floor. The main level was mostly used for social functions hosted by the College.

"I think it's a great idea. I've only been in Freeman Hall one time, but I can easily see it transformed into a newsroom. I wonder though, will the paper still be called *The Daily Courier*? Won't there be some sort of conflict with using the same name as before?"

The Provost chuckled and shook his head at Thomas. "Out of the mouth of babies. Or should I say, babes? I believe you have a point, Miss Ayres. But for now, I don't think that's our top concern. We have much bigger fish to fry before we have to worry about the name of the paper." He picked up his menu. "Speaking of fish, they serve a top-notch catfish plate here."

I felt the heat flood my face as I studied the menu. I wasn't sure if it was from the backward compliment I had received or the none-too-subtle criticism. Either was clearly intended to remind me of my youth and inexperience. I took a deep breath and promised myself to get Julie's therapist's number as soon as possible. It was time for me to dig into some of the issues that repeatedly sent me spiraling back into insecurity and self-doubt, which kept getting in the way of both my professional and personal life. What was the saying Ida shared with me? Something about how nobody can make you feel bad about yourself unless you let them. And by God, I was determined I wasn't going to let them anymore!

Chapter 30

It's amazing how quickly time passes when you're busy. Before I knew it, my first week as Thomas' assistant had ended, and I was facing a weekend that promised to be full of challenges. Jon phoned midweek to say he would be returning to Nashville on Friday, and he suggested he stop by to take me to dinner that evening. The prospect of seeing him again, but mostly of being alone with him, had me filled with a mixture of anxiety and anticipation that lasted the rest of the week. By the time Friday arrived, I could barely choke down a cup of coffee because the butterflies in my stomach seemed to have moved their way up into my throat. I wasn't sure how I was going to manage to eat dinner, especially considering who would be sitting at the table with me.

We arranged to meet at my apartment at 7 P.M. on Friday. I spent the hour before creating my usual pile of clothing discards in search of just the right outfit, eventually settling on a red turtleneck and black jeans. I thought the red color gave a boost to my pale complexion, and black jeans seemed to trim and elongate my already leggy lower body. I felt my long legs were my best physical feature, so I tried to emphasize them whenever I could. I finished the outfit with a pair of black ankle boots and turned my attention to trying to restore order to my clothing-tossed bedroom. I had just put away the last rejected item when I heard a knock on my door. Ebie, always the eager young lady when it came to visitors, beat me to the threshold and stood at attention waiting for me to open the door. Jon was holding a bouquet of flowers and a small box.

"Well! If it isn't my two favorite ladies!" His face broke into a huge smile as he looked from one to the other of us. My first thought was that he seemed to have grown even more handsome while he was away. I was momentarily struck speechless as I gawked at him. He was dressed in a pair of faded blue jeans and a white dress shirt topped by a black leather jacket. The word "delicious" immediately came to my mind. I felt myself flush with embarrassment as the image of him naked in my bed flashed through my mind. I stepped back to let him in, hoping to gather my wits about me before I sunk even further into a state of frazzled excitement. When I closed the door, and turned around, I saw he was staring at me with a bemused expression. Luckily, he must have decided to keep his thoughts to himself, because he remained silent as he held out the bouquet of flowers.

"These are for you, and this is for Ebie." His other hand produced the small box. At the sound of her name, Ebie began to dance at his feet.

"Thank you. I'll just put these in water." I accepted the bouquet from him and rushed into the kitchen, glad for an excuse to get away and attempt to calm my fluster. When I returned to the living room, he was sitting on the sofa with Ebie on his lap, carefully unwrapping the small box.

"I saw this one day when I was visiting my sister, and I just had to buy it for Ebie. Joan has two dogs and a cat, and I've seen how much fun they have playing with one just like this." He lifted a rubber ball from the box and shook it, causing it to jingle. "It's filled with small bells, but don't worry, the ball is very solid so there's no chance she could break it open and swallow one." He tossed it onto the floor and Ebie pounced on it and began batting it around the room excitedly, causing both of us to erupt in laughter. We stopped and looked at one another. Jon reached for my hand and deepened his gaze.

"I've really missed you. I hated to leave after everything that happened. I had no idea I would have to be gone so long." He lifted my hand to his mouth and pressed his warm lips against my palm. "Tell me how you've been? Has it been a difficult week?"

I could feel the blood rush to my head at the touch of his lips, followed by a tingle in a much lower region of my body. The sensation surprised me because it was still so new. I took a deep breath to try to calm myself. "It was helpful that I started my new job. I've been so busy I haven't had a lot of time to think about what has happened. Thomas has been wonderful. He's a whirlwind of activity, and he makes me laugh all the time."

Jon's smile was replaced by a frown at the mention of Thomas. I remembered how possessive he had been toward me whenever Thomas was around. Always keeping an arm around my shoulders or holding my hand, I hadn't given it much thought lately. I squeezed his hand gently.

"He's been a good friend and mentor. That's all."

He gave me a long look, as if he was considering what I said, then ducked his head slightly. "I'm not so sure he would describe his feelings toward you in exactly those terms. I saw the way he looked at you when he came here, and again at the hospital. I think he would like you to be much more than just his friend."

His suggestion surprised me. I hadn't sensed any special interest from Thomas. I remembered the day he invited Ida and me to dinner, and how I had thought she had been trying to set us up to be alone, but I had rejected that idea when I discovered how sick she'd been. If Thomas had any such thoughts about me, he had been doing a good job of hiding them.

"I think you're wrong, but even if you aren't, it doesn't matter because I don't feel that way about him."

A smile replaced his frown and he stepped forward to wrap me in his arms and place a gentle, but firm kiss on my lips. "I'm glad to hear that. But before we take this matter any further, perhaps we should leave for the restaurant. I promised you dinner, and I intend to keep my promise."

I was a little disappointed that he broke off our kiss so quickly, but I was relieved to have a little more time to adjust to being around him again. During the time we spent so many hours together, both at the hospital and at my apartment, I had grown, if not entirely comfortable, at least *used* to his presence. Since he'd been away, that feeling had been replaced by uncertainty. I knew the source of my feelings very likely had less to do with him than it did with me and my unresolved issues. Regardless of the reasons behind how I was feeling, I was jittery with the anticipation of having to address some things I had succeeded in keeping stuffed away for most of my life. Nonetheless, being close to him again, close enough to smell that wonderful combination of leather, cinnamon, and maleness, was making me anxious to dig up the source of my anxiety and loosen its hold on me.

He had made a reservation for us at *Jimmy Kelly's*, a local restaurant known for its steaks and clubby atmosphere. I always wanted to go there, but the prices kept me away. Jon didn't seem to have that concern. It was a treat to just sit back and allow him to order for me.

We spent the next hour digging into the best steak I had ever eaten, accompanied by a loaded baked potato and wedge salad, while we filled each other in on our week. I told Jon about my success at organizing Thomas' office and the odd lunch we shared with the Provost. He described the committee meetings he attended, where the business of relocating *The Daily Courier* was discussed. I learned by listening to him; this was a man of conviction and determination. When he believed in something, he held nothing back in his intent to bring it to fruition. I wondered if the same was true about his relationships. Would he be just as committed to seeing them through?

That question was still on my mind during the drive back to my apartment. Jon must have noticed my silence because, when he parked in front of my building, he turned in his seat and looked at me curiously.

"You've been awfully quiet since dinner. Did I bore you with my account of my work week?"

I shifted so I could face him. "Not at all. I've just been thinking about how determined you are at going after what you want. Have you always been that way?"

He leaned back against the door. "I suppose I have, though it hasn't always worked out to my advantage. The trick is to make sure you know what you really want before committing to going after it. Otherwise, you can find yourself in a situation that wasn't at all what you thought it would be."

I had heard some gossip about his earlier life, and I wondered if that was what he was thinking about. "Are you talking about your marriage?

He looked at me with surprise. "I didn't know you knew about that. I wanted to be the one to tell you, but I guess Nashville is a small town in that way." He rubbed his chin and stared out the window. "It happened when I was still pretty young; in my early twenties. She was the daughter of a business colleague of my father's and, truth be told, the marriage was kind of a set-up between the two of them. I guess they felt it would be a good idea, from a business standpoint. I was too eager to please my father at that time to pay much attention to how I felt. I later found out she was pretty much in the same boat. We made a go of it for a while, but finally the stress of putting on an act for the sake of our parents just got the better of us. She fell in love with an old high school sweetheart who wandered back into her life, so that was the end of that."

Even though it was clear he was trying to make light of what happened, I could hear the pain below the surface as he spoke. It made my heart go out to him. This was the Jon I had come to love. *Love*? There was that word again. I guess it was true. I had come to love him. It was because every now and then he would allow me to glimpse this layer of his complexity; the part of him that he kept hidden most of the time.

"That must have been tough. Was your father very upset with you?"

He grunted. "You could say that. He threatened to cut me out of the will if I didn't make things right with her. But he couldn't do anything about what she wanted, which was to leave me and marry her true love. He finally had to accept it was out of his hands. I guess you could say she got me off the hook, although at the time it didn't feel like a gift. The whole ordeal was pretty unpleasant."

His face was gently illuminated by the streetlight beside where we were parked, and I could see the pain in his face. "That helps me understand you better. I guess part of that shield you surround yourself with was put there to protect you from being hurt again. I would never want to cause you that kind of pain."

A look of surprise and pleasure crossed his face as he pulled me against his chest, wrapping his arms firmly around me. "You couldn't. You may not always know what you want, but your face shows every emotion you're experiencing. I would have to be pretty blind not to see if something was wrong."

I pulled back to look at him. "I had no idea I'm so easy to read. What am I feeling now?"

He looked down at me, his face twisted into a smirk. "You're trying to figure out whether or not you want me to stay the night."

"I guess you are pretty good at reading me. What I feel and what I think have been having a battle all night."

His eyes seemed to darken as he kept looking at me. "Then why not call a truce. What if we agree to just hold each other until we fall asleep? I promise not to push things any further than you're comfortable with.'

He seemed to be asking me to trust him but, truth be told, I wasn't sure if I trusted myself. Nonetheless, the idea of lying next to him again was appealing, and I didn't really want to send him home alone.

"I'm not sure this is such a good idea, but why don't you stay with me tonight? I like the idea of falling asleep in your arms."

His face broke into a big grin and he quickly opened the car door. "I thought you'd never ask!" He said with a laugh.

That night, true to his word, Jon held me against his chest until I fell asleep. I wasn't sure I would actually be able to sleep, given how fast my heart was beating. I must have been more tired than I realized because the next thing I knew the daylight was slipping in around the corners of my window blinds. I shifted so that I could look at the man who had served as my pillow, and found him looking at me through half-closed eyes.

"Good morning." His voice had a raspy quality and I wondered if he had slept at all.

I sat up, tucking the sheet under my arms. I had changed into a t-shirt and pajama bottoms before coming to bed, but for some reason, I suddenly felt naked being so close to him. "Morning. Would you like some coffee?"

He reached up and pulled me down onto the bed again, shifting so we were facing each other. "In a minute. Did you sleep well?"

I nodded slightly; hesitant to speak for fear my morning breath would offend him. I was trying to decide how I could discretely run to the bathroom for some mouthwash when I became aware of the rigid pressure against my belly where his torso met mine. He shifted so he was no longer touching me.

"Sorry. It's something that happens to men, whether we mean for it to or not. In this case, I have to admit I've been that way for most of the night."

I looked at him wide-eyed to see if he was joking. "That must have been uncomfortable," I said.

He smiled. "Kind of. But I was determined to keep my promise to you. It was worth it just to be able to hold you close again." He sat up and kissed the tip of my nose. "Now why don't you see about that coffee you mentioned and give me a few minutes to collect myself? It will be easier if you're not lying next to me."

Again, my heart and mind went to battle, with neither one coming out the clear winner. I was very tempted to pull back the covers, press myself against him and just let whatever happened, happen. But my mind shouted at me to get the hell up while I had the chance. I reluctantly scooted away from him. "Just so you know, I'm half-way tempted to stay right here and let nature take its course, but since I made such an issue about wanting you to just hold me, I guess the smartest thing for me to do is get up."

He sighed, propping his head on one arm. "I guess we're both in the same boat. As much as I would love to pull you back to bed and convince you to change your mind, the last thing I want to do is make you feel that I coerced you." He dropped back onto his back and closed his eyes. "Now run along and make that coffee. I'll be out in a minute."

I took one final look at him before heading to the kitchen. *Was I stupid or what?* What woman in her right mind would willingly walk away from the chance to be loved and made love to by a desirable, gorgeous, and increasingly sweet man? Yep. I had to be the biggest loon there ever was. I was getting increasingly frustrated with trying to figure out why I did the things I did, and it was starting to wear me out. Time for action, I decided. Today was the day for me to finally make that call to Julie's therapist so maybe the next time I found myself in a similar predicament, assuming I got the chance, I wouldn't have to struggle with knowing what I wanted. Jon had been pretty patient with me, so far, but I sure as hell didn't want to push my luck.

Chapter 31

Jon left after downing a quick cup of coffee, saying something about needing to make some phone calls and take care of some business. I couldn't help but feel he was a little too anxious to get away from me, but I was also glad not to draw out the goodbye. As soon as he left, I dug out the number Julie had given me and dialed her therapist. Since it was Saturday, I doubted anyone would answer but I decided to take a chance. I was about to hang up after hearing the phone ring four times when I heard a voice say hello. I waited for a recording telling me to leave a message when I realized the voice belonged to a live person who was asking me if anyone was there.

"Oh! Sorry! I didn't expect anyone to answer."

The person chuckled. "Would you like me to hang up so you can call back? I can let my machine pick up if you would prefer to talk to it."

There was that flush of embarrassment again. "No! I'm sorry. I just meant it occurred to me I might not reach anyone on a Saturday. I wanted to see about making an appointment with Dr. Blackburn. My friend, Julie Travers, recommended her."

"Oh, Julie! Such a wonderful young lady, and one of my favorite clients."

"You mean, you're Dr. Blackburn?"

I could hear her chuckle again. "I suppose it is a surprise that I would answer my own phone. Actually, you're right that I'm not usually in the office on Saturdays. My receptionist would normally take my calls during the week. I just happened to come in today to pick up some files, and I answered the phone on an impulse. You said you'd like to make an appointment?"

I nodded then realized she couldn't see me; a frequent habit of mine. "Yes, please. Julie speaks very highly of you. She thought it might be a good idea."

"What do you think? Is seeing me something you'd like to do?"

It felt like my therapy session had already started. "I believe so. I've been struggling with some things, and I'm hoping you can help me sort them out."

"I'll certainly try." I could hear her shuffling some papers. "I'm sorry, I didn't catch your name."

"It's Georgia. Georgia Ayres."

"Well, Georgia Ayres, what would you think about seeing me today? As I said, I'm not usually in the office on Saturday. But since I'm already here, I'd be willing to see you if you can come fairly soon. I have some things to do later this afternoon. Would, let's say, a half hour from now work for you?"

My heart jumped at the realization of what I was about to do. I hadn't expected things to happen so soon, but I guessed it was better to just dive right in, rather than mull around for days in my own anxiety. "That should work. Julie told me your office is somewhere near Hillsboro Village. I don't live too far from there."

"Yes. My office is at 3013 Belcourt Avenue. There's a small parking lot in front of the building. I'm in suite 201. Second floor. Let's meet at say, 10 o'clock?"

Again, the butterflies jumped from my stomach to my throat and I had to struggle to make my words come out. "Okay. I guess I'll see you then."

After I hung up, I had a small panic attack. *What had I done?* I was more than a little tempted to call her back and make up some excuse about why I couldn't see her today after all. I took a deep breath and pushed myself to take the plunge.

By the time I arrived at her office, I was practically faint with nerves. The door was locked, so I knocked quietly. Within seconds, a plump, middle-aged woman who stood a few inches shorter than I, opened the door. She was wearing jeans and a sweater, and her wavy, brown hair was pulled back into a ponytail. Her eyes regarded me warmly as she stood aside to let me enter the office.

"You must be Georgia. I'm Dr. Blackburn." She extended her hand in my direction,

I stared at it before reaching out to accept her handshake. We were standing in an outer reception area. There were a few chairs lined up against one wall with tables on each end that held a stack of magazines. A desk, which I assumed was intended for the missing receptionist, was placed adjacent to the chairs. A vase of drooping roses sat on top of the desk. A sign posted on the wall behind it read. "Please sign in and have a seat". I turned to look back at Dr. Blackburn and found her studying me carefully with a friendly look on her face.

"Let's go into my office? Normally, my receptionist would have you fill out a few forms, but we can take care of that later."

I followed her through a door to the left of the desk. Her office walls were painted a soft, golden yellow with white trim that reflected the sunlight streaming in from two windows located along one wall. Her desk was made of dark wood that appeared almost black. There were two chairs facing the desk made out of the same dark wood. The seat and back of the chairs were covered in yellow and white fabric that complemented the color of the walls. A small couch was placed against the wall to the right of the desk. A floor lamp stood to its left. A cocktail table sat in front of it, and an overstuffed chair had been placed at an angle to its right.

Dr. Blackburn walked to her desk, picked up a pad of paper and a pen, then turned to look at me. I noticed her eyes were a deep green that glowed with friendliness and a touch of mirth. She raised her hand and gestured down the length of her body. "I don't usually dress like this to meet clients, but as I said, I just popped in to pick up some files. Saturdays are usually devoted to family activities. In fact, I'll be heading to my son's soccer game when I leave here."

I nodded my understanding. "I appreciate you seeing me today." My eyes glanced at the various seating arrangements in the room. I had read that therapy sessions often took place with the client lying on a couch while the therapist sat nearby taking notes. I wondered if I would be expected to do the same. I guess Dr. Blackburn was as good at reading my thoughts as most everyone else in my life seemed to be because she answered my question before I could ask.

"Won't you sit over here?" She gestured to one of the two chairs facing her desk and moved to sit in the other one. "I like to spend the first session just getting to know a little about my new clients." She flipped open the notepad and settled back comfortably into the chair. "Why don't you start by telling me about your life: where you grew up, what your family is like, what you do for a living, anything you feel like sharing?"

For the next 45 minutes, I rambled; at least that's what I felt I was doing. I described what it had been like to grow up an only child with parents who seemed to barely notice me, except to point out one of my many shortcomings. It was a list that had grown long and weighty through my childhood and adolescence. As I spoke, I realized that escaping it was a driving force behind my decision to accept a job right out of high school in order to move out on my own. I told Dr. Blackburn about my experiences in school and the teacher who finally helped me find my voice. I also described how I met Julie in the school cafeteria. We both laughed at my description of how that had occurred. Finally, I told her about going to work for the *Nashville News* and everything that happened since then. I told her of my up and down interactions with Jon, my fast but short friendship with Ida that had ended with her sudden death, and the new job I had started at Belmont. There were a lot of details I omitted, either on purpose or because there just seemed to be too much to tell. Overall, I felt I was able to give her a pretty good idea of what my life had been like.

She had asked very few questions while I was talking. She mostly nodded making sympathetic sounds as she scribbled on her notepad. Occasionally, she made a perfunctory comment likely intended to let me know she was paying attention. When I finally reached the end of what I wanted to say, she looked at me warmly.

"That's quite an interesting story. Thank you for sharing it with me. Now, what I would like to ask you to do in the time we have left, is to tell me the one thing that pops into your mind first when I ask you to finish this statement: "My life would be so much better if…""

My answer came automatically. "I could stop being afraid."

She looked at me thoughtfully. "Okay. You've done great today, Georgia. I appreciate your willingness to share so much about your life with me. It's a good start. I suggest we plan to see each other weekly for a while. I checked my appointment book before you arrived. It appears I have an opening every Monday at 5:30 P.M. Does that time work with your schedule?"

I was struck for a moment by something she said: "A good start". I mean, really, a *start*? I felt as though I had just emptied out my guts to her. I couldn't imagine there was much more I could say.

I was still mulling this over when I realized she was waiting for my reply. "Oh. Umm, yes. Monday at 5:30 should be fine. I leave work around 5, so that would give me enough time to get here."

"Good. Now I'd like to give you something to take home with you that I want you to think about before our next session." She reached into her desk drawer, pulled out a small paper card and handed it to me. "Don't read it yet. I want you to carve out some time when you can be alone in a quiet environment. Then take it out and spend some time thinking about what it says. It might even be helpful for you to write down your reactions, especially since writing is your chosen profession. We'll talk about it when I see you next week. Actually, our next session is in two days. Normally, I wouldn't suggest meeting again so soon, but I think it will be good this time."

I followed her numbly out of her office to the door leading out of the reception area. She opened the door and stood aside so I could get by. "Take care, Georgia. I'll see you Monday."

I headed quickly to where my car was parked. All of a sudden, I felt a sense of urgency to get away as quickly as I could. I wasn't sure why, but I didn't want to take the time to figure it out either. I just knew the sooner I could put the last hour out of my mind the better.

I drove to the end of Belcourt Avenue, deciding on a whim to turn right instead of going left, which would have been the most direct route to my apartment. In a few minutes, I found myself pulling up in front of the house where Ida had lived. I parked on the curb in front and sat staring at the brick house. The flower gardens that Ida had been so proud of looked sadly neglected. The grass was at least 3 inches too tall. As I sat looking at the house, I felt a sense of expectation. It suddenly occurred to me that I was waiting for Ida to appear on her doorstep to invite me in. I knew that wasn't going to happen, but the mind likes to take its own path sometimes.

I made my way to her front steps. The curtains that draped the sitting room windows had been left open, and I was surprised to see her furniture was still as I remembered it from the time I had visited her to talk about my idea for relocating the *Courier*. As far as I could tell, nothing seemed to have been moved. I wondered if Beth was planning on selling the house furnished, or if perhaps she was considering moving into it with her family. I thought the latter was unlikely, since I had the impression she was fully entrenched in her life in New York. But I thought it was odd that she wouldn't want to take some of Ida's things back home with her.

I turned and walked back across the yard to *Tweedledee*. A heaviness had moved into my heart, and I suddenly felt like crying. Ida was gone. My first job had ended badly. I may have ruined things with Jon because of my hesitation toward him. Now I had embarked on a journey of self-discovery that would take me who knew where.

You certainly have a way of getting yourself into messes, I thought to myself. That was the one sure thing I could say was true.

Chapter 32

It was the next day before I remembered the card Dr. Blackburn had given me. I spent the rest of Saturday running errands and cleaning my apartment; tasks designed to distract me from thinking about the things I really needed to do. To be honest, I was procrastinating. But at least, I admitted it to myself.

Julie had phoned me midday to ask me to go for a walk, but I begged off, telling her I had a lot of things to get done before the beginning of the workweek. The reality was I was avoiding her because I knew we'd end up talking about my conversation with Dr. Blackburn, and I just wasn't ready to open that can of worms just yet.

When Sunday rolled around, I had procrastinated myself into a deep funk, because I hadn't succeeded in relieving my mind of what was weighing it down. I filled a bowl of food for Ebie, turned on the coffee pot, and made a quick slice of toast with peanut butter, then carried my breakfast into the living room. The day was overcast with heavy, gray clouds that carried the scent of rain, which matched my mood perfectly. I settled onto the sofa and crossed my legs, pulling a blanket over me to cut the chill in the air. The coffee was warm going down my throat and I could feel the warmth spreading into my chest.

While I was munching on my peanut butter toast, which had become my go-to breakfast ever since Jon introduced me to it, I finally allowed myself to review my session with Dr. Blackburn. It really wasn't that big of a deal when I thought back over the things I said to her. Not unless you consider revealing some of the most intimate details of your life to a stranger a big deal, which I did. I found myself wondering what she thought of me, which was a large part of my cloudy mood. I was worried whether she liked me, and if I seemed like a silly girl in describing the details of my life.

That seemed to be par for my course; always wondering what someone else thought of me, and whether they found me good enough. *But good enough for what?* I wondered. *To be loved? To be worthy of their attention?* I knew I had a tendency to try to make everyone happy and realized my desire for approval must be at the core of that behavior. But I also knew I had been taking big strides. Well, baby steps really; toward becoming more forthright. Hadn't I stood up for myself at work? Well, no, I had actually snuck off with my virtual tail-between-my-legs after I was fired. Hadn't I voiced my opinion to the Provost? Yes, that was true, but I still blushed with embarrassment at his reaction. Although I had been honest with Jon about my inexperience and desire to sleep with him, I had eventually backtracked my way into a state of doubt, causing me to pull back from the newfound intimacy we established. The truth was, I seemed to wobble on every issue of importance to me. I would take one step forward in my goal of becoming more secure and independent, then stumble two steps back as I let fear get the best of me.

It was then I remembered the card Dr. Blackburn had given me. I tucked it into the back pocket of my jeans before I left her office. I hustled over to where I hung them in the closet. I settled back onto the couch and looked at it curiously. The card was colored a deep orange with white lettering that read *Life isn't supposed to make you feel good, or to make you feel bad, either.*

Life is just supposed to make you feel. There was no author listed for the quote. I read it through again and considered what it meant.

Maybe the message on that card got to the essence of my fear. I was worried I was never going to be happy because there always seemed to be something that came along to shake things up every time they seemed to be going reasonably well. Maybe the problem was that I expected life to be a constant state of happiness. When it wasn't, I chalked it up to some shortcoming on my part.

I was suddenly startled out of my mental ramblings by the sound of papers splattering onto the floor as Ebie jumped up onto the coffee table in front of my sofa. I tossed the mail there the previous evening after returning from my therapy session and had forgotten about it in my self-absorbed state. I reached down to gather it into a pile, and a manila envelope caught my eye. I laid the rest of the stack at the other end of the table from where Ebie had eventually settled, and ran my finger carefully under the flap of the envelope. The cover sheet bore the letterhead of a local law firm. I scanned down the page quickly and felt my breath catch at what I read. There was also a light blue envelope the cover sheet indicated had been written by Ida to me. I sat that aside to read back through the official letter to satisfy myself it really did say what I first thought it said. I jumped from the sofa and ran to the kitchen to grab the phone.

Julie answered on the third ring and I rattled off a mostly incoherent response to her greeting.

"Whoa, Georgia! Take a breath, then try that again. All I got was something about a house and a will."

I forced myself to take a couple of deep breaths in an attempt to slow myself before speaking again. "Ida left me her house. I got a letter from a lawyer stating she left it to me in her will. Apparently, she had him draw up a revision to it a couple of weeks ago. She left me the whole thing; furniture and furnishings, except for a few family heirlooms she indicated should be given to Beth. A house, Julie! Can you believe that?"

"Wow! That's amazing. She must have really cared for you. Of course, it was obvious she did from everything you've told me about your relationship with her. But to leave you her house means she regarded you as family. That's really special."

I had been leaning against the kitchen counter while she spoke. As the reality of what she said sunk in I allowed myself to slide down so I was sitting on the floor. "What am I supposed to do with a house?"

"I guess the first question is; can you afford it? Did the letter say whether or not there's a mortgage you'd have to assume? If it didn't, I'm sure someone at the bank could help you sort it out. I can ask Harry if you want."

Harry was her boyfriend and the assistant branch manager at the bank where she worked. Apparently, their relationship had been going strong for some time and I felt a moment of regret to realize I had spent so little time asking her about it. I promised myself I would remedy that as soon as possible.

"The letter says it's totally paid off. She even arranged for the property taxes for the next year to be paid in advance so I wouldn't have to worry about that for a while." I paused as I let my hands move to the small envelope I had yet to open. "There's something else, too. Ida apparently wrote me a private letter that was included with the official letter from the lawyer. I'd like to read it to you, if that's okay."

Julie quickly agreed, so I carefully opened the envelope and unfolded the two sheets it contained. After taking a deep breath, I began to read.

My dearest Georgia:

I know when you receive this letter you will already be in a state of shock from the events that led up to it being delivered to you. I have known for some time that my health is declining and the heart condition I was born with will soon cause my life to end. Please forgive me for not telling you, but I wanted our time together to be free of the cloud of impending death that tends to hang around whenever news of ones' mortality becomes blatantly evident.

Getting to know you has been one of the joys of my life. You have been a surprise to this old lady, one that has brought laughter to my days and warmth to my heart. If I had been fortunate enough to be a mother, I would have wished for a daughter with the spunk and spirit you have always displayed to me. I know you will shake your head at my describing you in that way, but the truth is; you are stronger than you think you are. The only thing holding you back from realizing your strength is self-doubt. It is my wish for you to you allow yourself to cast that aside and embrace self-love instead.

Since you're reading this letter, it also means you are now aware I have left you my house and most of its contents. Beth will receive a few personal items which have been in our family for many years and should remain so. The rest is yours to do with as you please. I will not impose any expectation on what you decide to do with my gift, but it is my hope you will bring life to it again. Perhaps it will be a good place to raise your own family someday, and in that regard, I hope you will open your mind and your heart to the man who has been seeking a place there.

I have been aware for some time of the depth of feelings that have been brewing between you and Jon. Though I had misgivings about him at the start, I do believe he is sincere in his intentions toward you. Do not be afraid to love, my dear girl. Allow yourself to be loved in return. I realize that means you will have to open yourself up to being vulnerable, but nothing worth having comes without the price of letting go of at least a little of the false security we delude ourselves into trusting.

Lastly, I hope you will work hard to make sure our dream for the relocation of The Daily Courier comes to fruition. I have every faith it will work out as we have intended. It will be a move I would be proud of, and one that will bring honor to the memory of my aunt. Use the expertise and guidance that Thomas can offer you, and do not mistake his playful manner for a lack of *steadfastness. He will be a powerful compatriot in this battle, and one who you can follow without fail.*

Be brave, dear girl. Know that I will be watching over you for the rest of your life.

Love,
Ida

Tears had begun to flow steadily down my cheeks as I read the letter, and I allowed a sob to escape as I reached the end. I sat down the phone so that I could blow my nose and I momentarily forgot about it until I heard the faint sound of Julie's voice over the receiver.

"I'm sorry. I put the phone down for a minute so I didn't hear what you just said."

"I said I'm coming over. Stay put, I'll be there in ten minutes."

I nodded at the phone and hung it up. I was still sitting on the floor staring at the letter from Ida when I heard a knock on my door. I opened it expecting to find Julie and was surprised instead to see Jon. His hands were jammed into the pockets of his black jeans and he smiled at me nervously when I opened the door.

"Jon! I wasn't expecting you. I was just talking to Julie. She said she was coming over."

He pushed past me into my apartment. "I know, I ran into her outside. She said she was on her way to see you. She said you'd had some rather earthshaking news. I convinced her to let me come up here to see you first, and she asked me to tell you she'll be by a little later." He looked at me steadily. "I hope you aren't disappointed to see me."

Before I could answer him, the tears I had successfully staunched a few minutes earlier began to gush forth again. He quickly stepped forward and pulled me into a tight embrace. To my relief, he did not speak or ask me to explain what I was feeling. Instead, he just held me silently and kissed my head until my tears began to subside. When I finally felt I could cry no more, I took a deep breath and allowed myself to relax into his embrace. We stood that way for a long minute before I felt him gently pull back from me. When I glanced up, he was looking at me intently, as if he was seeking an answer to a question he had not asked. I suddenly realized the question had been there all along. He did not need to speak the words out loud. I reached my arms up so my hands were clasped behind his neck and smiled at him shyly. "Yes."

His eyebrows lifted in question as he looked closely at me. "Yes? Does that mean what I think it does?"

I tightened my grip around his neck and smiled up at him. "Yes, I want to be with you, and yes, I'm ready to go wherever that takes us."

His face lit up with what can only be described as joy mixed in with a hearty dose of relief. "Thank God. I was afraid Ida's death would make you run away from me. I know how hard it is for you to trust me, and I know how scared you've been that you would end up hurt. I was afraid the pain of losing your friend would push you into a deep hole of despair and self-doubt." He frowned at me. "I'm almost afraid to ask, but what happened? You seem changed in some significant way."

I took his hand and led him to the sofa. When we were sitting facing each other, I began to speak. I described how my fear of losing him had given me the courage to phone Dr. Blackburn to begin the process of self-discovery. I told him about the card she had given me and how it helped me realize I had been defeating any chance I had of happiness by expecting my life to be smooth sailings all the time. When it wasn't, I tended to chalk it up to some imperfection on my part. I showed him the letter I received from the lawyer and the personal note from Ida. When he finished reading them, he looked at me and I was surprised to see his eyes glistening with tears.

"This is all so amazing. A lot has happened to you in the past two days." He leaned back against the sofa shaking his head. "I'm not sure I would be handling it as well as you seem to be."

I took his hand in mine. "Another thing I've realized is that I don't have to be perfect. It's okay for me to show it when I'm feeling uncertain and vulnerable." He folded both of my hands in his and waited for me to continue. "I'm not really handling things as well as it might appear on the surface, but I feel like I can get a grip on things eventually with the help of Dr. Blackburn." I hesitated as I lifted my head to look at him, "and you." That is, if you're willing to take a chance on me, even after you've seen first-hand what a mess I can make of things."

A grin spread across his face as he held my hands more tightly. "I wouldn't have it any other way. Your unpredictability is one of the first things that attracted me to you. Well, that, and your uncanny knack for always ending up in the middle of a messy situation."

I laughed in agreement. "It does seem I find myself stumbling into uncomfortable circumstances more often than I want to admit. But maybe the tide is turning on that, too." I held up the letter from the lawyer. "Want to take a ride with me? Check out Ida's house and help me figure out what I want to do about it? I'd like to call Julie and ask her to meet us there, too."

"It would be my pleasure. But only if you scoot over here and give me a kiss before we go."

I lost no time in doing exactly what he suggested. The kiss started out sweet and soft but I could feel the heat of our stirred passion beginning to kindle as it deepened. Just when I was reconsidering my idea of leaving the apartment, Jon pulled back from me.

"I think we should go. Not that I wouldn't love to continue down the path that we seem to be heading, but I want to wait for the right time." He stood and pulled me with him. "Plus, I'm selfishly hoping if I leave you wanting more, your desire will build until you just won't be able to resist me."

I leaned into him and tried to slow my heartbeat that had begun to patter rapidly as we kissed. "I don't think you'll have to worry about that. I doubt I'll be able to think about anything else until we can be alone again." I looked up at him with an impish grin. "In fact, maybe I shouldn't call Julie. I seem to recall that Ida has a rather comfy sofa. Perhaps we should try it out."

His eyebrows raised in surprise. "Who are you and what did you do with Georgia? If one session of therapy has made this much of a difference in you, I can't wait to see what happens after several more." He turned me so my back was to him then gently pushed me toward the kitchen. "Call Julie so we can go check out your new home. I did promise her I wouldn't keep you all to myself the rest of the day. Besides, the sooner we leave, the sooner we can come back."

Chapter 33

The letter from the lawyer included a key to the front door of Ida's house. Julie pulled up at the same time Jon and I did. I unlocked the door and stepped into the foyer. The three of us stood silently for a minute, glancing around the space that was eerily silent, yet somehow seemed to vibrate with an unseen energy. I had only been in Ida's house once, but the memory of that day came to mind with a force that had me reaching for the hall table to steady myself. Jon came up behind me and put an arm around my shoulders. "You're not alone. We're here with you every step of the way."

Julie appeared on my left and nodded her agreement. "Take it as slow as you need to. There's no rush."

I pulled myself upright, bolstered by the strength of their support, and walked to the sitting room where Ida served me tea and sandwiches. The room was bathed in the light of the late afternoon sun, which made everything appear golden. I ran my hand over the table that held the phone she used to talk to Thomas and noticed it was covered in a faint coating of dust. I turned back into the foyer and crossed to the other side to enter a room containing a formal dining table and chairs. A buffet held an assortment of china and glass wear. I noticed there were a few bare spots where it was obvious that certain items had been recently removed, since the vacated spaces were free of the dust that ringed the other items. I guessed these must have been part of the family treasures that had been given to Beth.

A door at the back of the dining room led to a kitchen. It was surprisingly large and contained a small table with two chairs placed beneath a window that provided a view of a small side yard. The rest of the space contained the usual assortment of appliances and a bookshelf with several well-worn cookbooks. To the rear of the kitchen was a door that opened into a small mudroom with a washer and dryer. A second door at the rear of the house led to a decent sized back yard, which, to my delight, contained a brick patio decked out with an umbrella table, four chairs, and two lounge chairs. A small round table had been placed between the two lounge chairs. I was seized with the image of us luxuriating in the midday sun, icy beverages melting on the table between us, Ebie dozing in her own pool of sunlight. I could even picture Julie and her steady boyfriend, Harry, laughing at some shared joke while resting under the shade of the umbrella.

"Nice!" I hadn't heard Julie walk up behind me. I turned to smile at her.

"Yes. I was just imagining all of us sitting out here. I even pictured Harry with us."

Her eyebrows lifted in question. "Really? I'm surprised you thought of him. I mean, I've certainly talked about him enough in the past to make you aware of how interested I am in him. But it's been some time since he's come up in a conversation."

I frowned at her gentle rebuke. "I'm afraid I've been so wrapped up in myself, and my real or imagined life dramas, I haven't been a very good friend. I hope you'll give me a chance to make it up to you."

She waved a hand as if to say it wasn't an issue. "Don't worry about it. I'm sure the day will come when the tables will be turned. Let's just say you'll owe me one."

"It's more accurate to say I'll owe you a bunch of ones."
I wrapped my arms around her in a grateful hug. "Thank you for always being so understanding."

"Hey! Can I get in on that?" Jon must have been waiting out of sight for our private moment to end because he unexpectedly walked up and enclosed both of us in a snug embrace. It was a sweet moment that had me again, close to tears. But this time, the tears would have been of joy.

I pulled back and looked at the two people who I realized meant more to me than anyone else ever had in my entire life. "Ready to see the rest of the house?" When they eagerly agreed, I led the way back inside, through the kitchen to an arched doorway that led to the hall behind the foyer. There were two doors that opened off the rear of the hallway, one of which contained a substantial pantry where canned goods and paper products were stored. The other revealed what used to be known as a powder room. Because it was where ladies would steal away to check their makeup and powder the shine off their noses. These days it was just called a half-bath since it only contained a toilet and sink instead of the usual bathtub.

A staircase rose from the end of the foyer to the second floor, which was not a full floor but designed more like an attic. Nonetheless, it contained a small bedroom at the back and a large master bedroom at the front, with a good-sized bathroom between the two with doors that opened from either room. The smaller bedroom only had enough space for a single bed, dresser, desk and chair. The master bedroom was large enough for a four-poster bed, bedside tables and lamps, an overstuffed chair with a matching hassock, a floor lamp for reading, a chest of drawers, and a dressing table with a stool. There was a bay window across the front with a padded bench built into the alcove it created.

Ida's touch had been evident throughout the entire house, but it was especially so in this room. I found myself drawn to it in some inexplicable way. I imagined curling up with a good book in the bay window while Jon sat nearby reading the newspaper with Ebie snuggled on his lap. As soon as that image had crossed my mind, it was replaced with another that involved the comfortable looking bed. I quickly turned toward the window before anyone else could read my thoughts. I must not have turned quickly enough, because Jon walked up behind me and pressed his body against mine, causing me to struggle to catch my breath as the heat instantly rose between us.

"Ahem. Do you want me to leave?" Julie stood hesitantly in the doorway looking at us.

"Yes." "No!" Jon and I both spoke at once but with opposite answers, eliciting a chuckle from Julie.

"I'll take that as a *maybe*, which gives me the right to stay exactly where I am for the time being." She walked to where we stood, still pressed against each other and gazed out the window. "This is such a nice place, Georgia. It's simple, but full of warmth and comfort. I can definitely see you being happy here."

I looked at her with surprise. "You can? I haven't decided yet whether I should keep the house or sell it."

"Are you sure? I haven't seen you look so content since…well, I've never seen you look this content."

I looked at Jon. "What do you think? Would it be crazy for me to keep the house? I mean, it's awfully big for one person."

Jon smiled at me warmly. "Ida was one person, and it seems she was quite happy here. Besides, you'll have Ebie for company, and I'm sure you can find other ways to fill these rooms." He looked at me pointedly.

"I'll need to talk with the lawyer. I'm not sure I understand how all of this is supposed to work. I mean, I know Ida left it to me, but I don't know what other expenses are involved in owning a house." I looked at Jon. "Will you go with me to talk to him? Maybe you can help me make sense of it all."

"Of course, I will. Let's give him a call when we get back to your apartment and set up a meeting. I also want to phone Thomas so I can check on the progress of our project."

I smiled. "Our project. I like the sound of that. You know, there was a time when I thought you were the enemy in all of this." I shook my head in disbelief. "I couldn't have been more wrong."

"I didn't exactly give you a lot of reason to trust me. It took me a while to realize you and I were on the same side. By then, I had already started developing strong feelings for you. Frankly, I wasn't sure what to do about any of that, so I'm certain I was giving off mixed signals." He pulled me to him again. "I'm just glad I didn't chase you off before I had a chance to figure it out."

Julie had been standing close by watching our exchange and I looked over to find her smiling smugly. "It seems to me both of you have been struggling with the same ambivalence. I'm just glad you finally seem to be figuring it out." She glanced at her watch. "Oh! I have to go! I promised to meet Harry for an early dinner and I need to go home to change first." She looked at the two of us with a slight frown. "Say, why don't the four of us get together sometime next week? I'd like you to get to know Harry, and I'd like him to meet you, Jon."

Jon looked at me for confirmation and I nodded. "Sounds good to me. Why don't you and Georgia set something up? I'll be around all next week, so anytime will work for me."

We hurried down the staircase and opened the front door for Julie. As we stood side-by-side, arms wrapped around each other's waist, watching her as she drove away, something Ida had once said came to my mind. We had been talking about being strong and having the courage to act on our convictions. She said, "We just have to get out of our own way sometimes". At that moment, I realized how very true her words were. I had been getting in my own way for a long time, but I was finally beginning to learn how to step around my fear.

Chapter 34

The day couldn't have been more perfect for a party. It was the Fourth of July. The weather Gods had decided to temporarily spare Nashville from their usual scorching hot, humid, mosquito-ridden assault, and instead hand over a day that was comfortably warm, with a steady breeze and no chance of rain. Centennial Park, located in the heart of the city, and the home of the only existing replica of the original Parthenon in Athens, Greece, was decked out in a colorful array of banners welcoming everyone to the Fourth of July festivities. A stage had been placed along the east end of the Parthenon to hold the various musical acts expected. Several tents had been raised to provide shade and shelter for food vendors and arts and crafts sellers who rented space for the occasion. A dozen or so rows of chairs were being set up in front of the stage. A line-up of portable toilets, commonly referred to as *porta-potties*, had been placed off to the side of the road that circled the Parthenon.

Several dozen attendees had already arrived and were busy claiming their spots with lawn chairs or blankets. Julie and I decided to come ahead of the rest of our group in order to snag one of the picnic tables scattered around the grounds. We were lucky to find one that had a clear view of the stage, but set a little out of the way of where most of the crowd would be congregating. Jon and Harry would be arriving together a little later with a portable grill and a cooler full of everything we would need for our picnic dinner. Of course, we had given them a detailed list of everything they should bring, so we could make sure we didn't end up with several bags of chips and nothing to go with them.

Jon and Harry had become fast friends after our double date the week after Julie, Jon and I toured Ida's house. I still thought of it as Ida's house even though Ebie and I moved into it the first of June. Moving had been much less of an ordeal than I anticipated because the apartment I had been living in came furnished. As a result, it was just a matter of packing-up some household things I purchased on my own, my books, and the contents of my closets. I gave notice to my landlord the beginning of May, allowing me ample time to box up my meager possessions. Throughout the entire ordeal, Ebie stood sentinel at the front door as if to say "I don't know what you're up to, but you're not going anywhere without me!"

Once we arrived at the house, Ebie rushed around from room to room until she finally chose her spot on the window seat in the master bedroom, turning around in a circle before collapsing with a sigh after which she immediately fell asleep. The rest of us; Jon, Julie, Harry, Thomas, and Mary Alice, the ER nurse who had apparently become more than just a friend to Thomas, lugged in the boxes and tried to avoid knocking into each other as we passed in and out of the front door.

When all of the boxes had been unloaded, the six of us plopped on the patio to wait for the delivery of the pizzas I ordered. Luckily, *Shakey's Pizza Parlor* had added delivery services the previous month, so all we had to do was pop open some drinks and relax. It was the first time we had all been in the same place, at the same time. I looked around the group curiously to see if I could gauge how things were going. I noticed Julie and Harry looked perfectly comfortable snuggled onto one of the lounge chairs, her back fitting neatly against his chest as his legs straddled her sides. Ever since I had become aware of how self-absorbed I'd become, to the extent that I had been virtually oblivious that my best friend had fallen in love, I'd been making a conscious effort to pay more attention to what was going on with her. By the looks on their faces whenever they were in the same room together, I would have to say there was a lot going on. Julie seemed blissfully happy.

Thomas and Mary Alice pulled two chairs next to where Julie and Harry sat and were trading quips about who carried more boxes during the move. Discovering the two of them were together had been a nice surprise. After my foreboding paranoia that Ida had been trying to set up Thomas and me, it was a relief to discover his attention had been totally turned towards catching Mary Alice's eye. From what I could gather from some of the comments she made, she'd had her eye on him for some time. But it took the sad turn of events at the hospital to put them in the right place at the right time for sparks to ignite.

According to Mrs. Stayhill, who had turned out to be a wealth of knowledge on all of the intricate goings-on around the office and the Belmont campus as a whole, Thomas and Mary Alice had been pretty much inseparable since the day of Ida's funeral service. It was certainly an odd way for a relationship to start, but I liked to think Ida had a hand in it. As far as what she had in mind for Thomas and me, I decided she just wanted us to become good friends. Perhaps the thought of that happening gave her some comfort as she realized her own life was rapidly approaching the end.

I turned toward the house as I heard the backdoor slam, and was pleased to see Jon carrying a tray laden with iced beverages and bottles of beer, which he proceeded to distribute to everyone. Once Jon realized Thomas posed no threat when it came to his interest in me, the two of them reached an unspoken truce that allowed them to join forces in their mutual quest to see through the relocation of the *Courier* to Belmont. The two of them had been spending quite a bit of time pouring over the details of the move. While I couldn't go so far as to call them friends, there was, at least, a friendly aspect to their interactions.

When it became clear the project was going to move ahead with only a few manageable wrinkles, Jon arranged to be relocated full-time to Nashville in the role of manager/consultant for the Barnett Corporation. His job was really just to make sure the corporation's interests were being protected. However, the more deeply involved he became in the day-to-day activities of the move, the more he seemed to become engrossed in understanding the actual mechanics of running a newspaper and developing a curriculum to match its production. With his family's long-standing involvement in newspaper publishing, I was not surprised to find he was more enthralled by the production side of things, which worked out perfectly because that left the curriculum development to Thomas' able hands.

As soon as the funding fell into place, my role had also shifted from Thomas' assistant to that of feature writer and instructor. That meant I got to keep doing what I most loved to do…write stories about the quirky and entertaining things people in Nashville were up to. On top of that, I was actually going to be paid to talk to students about how to break out of the hard-news format of writing in order to tell stories in a more creative and compelling way. That also meant I was going to have a chance to learn more about the *New Journalism* approach Thomas had been trying to spearhead into the Nashville newspaper scene. I was still in the infancy stage of understanding exactly what that style of journalism involved, but I could see it was clearly a way of moving things past a staid, often boring, method of reporting the news.

As for Jon and me, well, we were still a work-in-progress. I continued my weekly therapy sessions with Dr. Blackburn and made great strides toward figuring out what had turned me into such a scaredy-cat. Not that my fear had disappeared, but it was a milder version of what I'd been living with for most of my life. Jon rented a small place near the Belmont campus. It was really nothing more than a bedroom with an attached bath and a small kitchenette, but, as he explained to me, he didn't really plan on spending all that much time there; a fact that both excited and terrified me.

Fear was still a constant companion of mine. It hadn't caused me to hightail it away from him, which would have been my usual response to his barely disguised hint he planned to spend a lot of time with me. In the four weeks since I moved into the house, he spent more nights there than at his own apartment. It was a situation I wasn't totally comfortable with, given the conservatism drilled into me as a child. But the more I was around him, the more I could feel him chipping away at those precepts. After all, I told myself, I had Ida's blessing.

The Belmont paper project, as we had fallen into the habit of referring to it, was well on its way to becoming a reality. The new wing was nearly complete. The space we wished for in Freeman Hall had been renovated and was just waiting for its inhabitants to arrive. Basically, we were all glad to take a breath and kick back for a while, after all of the tension and worries that had surrounded the project since its inception. July was going to be our downtime, at least in principle. The truth was that after the Independence Day party, we would all probably find ourselves gravitating toward the campus to see what else needed to be done. The project was our collective baby, and we were each eager to make sure it was well nurtured.

By the time Jon and Harry arrived at Centennial Park for the Independence Day festivities, Julie and I had covered the table with a red, white, and blue cloth, then placed a ring of anti-mosquito candles around the perimeter. Thomas and Mary Alice had promised to bring a second cooler with icy drinks, including a contraband container of gin and tonic we had all mutually agreed was worth the possible risk of discovery by the local police force. Nashville had come a long way from its days as a dry town where alcohol was only available in the back room of liquor stores. But it still wasn't legal to consume it in public. To get around the issue, Mary Alice came up with the idea of pouring it into a large plastic jug with a flip top that allowed it to be easily poured into our red and blue plastic cups.

The crowd had been growing as Julie and I worked at preparing our space. I decided to climb up on one of the picnic table benches to see if I could spot Jon and Harry. Luckily, they were just making their way through the crowd, so I waved to catch their attention. I was just about to climb down from the bench when I also noticed Thomas and Mary Alice making a beeline for our table.

"Well, it seems everybody is here now." I hoped off the bench and smiled happily at Julie.

"It's great, isn't it? Being happy and hopeful, knowing whatever life throws at us next, we're surrounded by good friends to help us through. Good times or bad, it's going to be alright."

"It is, isn't it? I think I believe that now."

She wrapped me in a hug. "I never had any doubt, although I have to admit, my resolve to stay optimistic was beginning to wear a little thin as I watched you beat yourself up with worry over and over again."

"Ida used to tell me that I was stronger than I realized. I guess she was onto something."

Julie gave me a comical look. "Ya think?"

I was just about to answer her with some pointed retort when I was lifted off my feet. Jon had grabbed me from behind and was in the process of twirling me around, barely missing knocking the cooler of drinks out of Thomas' hands as he walked up behind us.

"Hey! Watch it, Pal. I'm carrying precious cargo here!" Thomas said as he broke into a fit of laughter that was quickly echoed by Mary Alice.

Jon set me on my feet and turned me around to look at him. "So am I, Thomas. So am I." His gaze took on an intensity that quickly had me blushing with embarrassment. That was something I still hadn't managed to make any headway at changing, but I decided to accept that it was just part of me.

"Um. I think I could use something cold to drink." I was feeling a little shaky on my feet and I placed my hands-on Jon's arms to steady myself.

Mary Alice nudged Thomas who quickly sat the cooler down. The two of them lined up six cups and filled each with the gin and tonic, adding a slice of lime before passing them around. When we were all holding a cup of the enticing beverage, Harry raised his in the air. "I have an announcement to make." He stopped and glanced at Julie. "Actually, WE have an announcement to make." The two of them stood grinning at each other while the rest of us waited in anticipation.

"Well?" I said. "What's the big announcement?"

Harry nodded at Julie who took a deep breath. "We're getting married! Harry asked me last night, but I wanted to wait until we were all together before we said anything."

There was a moment of stunned silence quickly followed by the mingled sounds of laughter, applause, and congratulations. Everyone was trying to speak at once as we each stepped forward to offer hugs and well wishes. When we settled enough to remember our drinks, I looked into my cup for a moment before lifting it in their direction. "To Julie and Harry; the best friend a person could ever hope for, and the man who won her heart. May your lives together be full of joy."

Everyone added their cheers and took long sips of the drinks before going about the task of setting up the rest of the picnic. Jon and Harry placed a small grill just outside the ring of bug candles so the smoke would blow away from our picnic table. Mary Alice, Julie, and I dug the rest of the food out of the cooler and laid out the buns, condiments, chips, pickles, and watermelon slices that would round out our meal. Thomas pulled out an array of funny hats bearing red, white, and blue streamers and stars, and passed them around. The rest of the afternoon and evening went smoothly. Everybody seemed to be having a good time. There was a lot of laughter as Thomas and Mary Alice kept us in stitches with their comical banter. Apparently, they were well matched, and it made me smile to imagine what Ida would have said if she could see them together.

At one point, Julie and I found ourselves with a few minutes alone while the others set off to explore the vendor tents, or take their place in the never-ending *porta-potty* lines. We sat next to each other at the table and Julie turned so she could face me. "I hope you don't mind that I didn't tell you first. I wanted to, but Harry convinced me I should wait."

I chuckled. "I guess he was worried I wouldn't be able to keep it a secret. You know, my poker face, and all."

She nodded sheepishly. "I guess so." She frowned and looked down at her hand that displayed the engagement ring she had kept hidden away in her purse until after their announcement. "I was hoping you'd agree to be my maid of honor."

A big grin burst out on my face and I had to clear my throat of the emotion causing it to close up. When I finally managed to speak, my words came out like a squeak.

Julie leaned closer to me and asked, "What did you just say? It sounded like you said I'm an ass."

I shook my head furiously and swiped at the tears that had begun to course down my cheeks. "No, silly! I said I was hoping you'd ask."

We leaned our foreheads against each other and laughed in relief. Finally, I pulled back and looked at her quizzically. "When? You didn't say when you plan to get married?"

"Probably October. We'd like to have an outdoor wedding. I want to wait until the weather is a little cooler. I was thinking of asking you what you thought about having the reception on your patio. I know it's not very large, but we've decided to only invite our families and closest friends, so it should be just big enough."

I smiled with delight as my mind began to turn over the possibilities. "I'd love it. At least, you're giving me a few months to sort out the details."

Julie leaned forward and hugged me with a laugh. "I know that look. You're already thinking about how you'll decorate.

Promise me you won't go crazy. We really just want to keep things simple."

I smiled at her mischievously. "I promise you; it will be perfect."

"You're impossible, you know."

"I know. You wouldn't have it any other way."

The rest of our group had begun to meander back, so we scooted closer together to make room for Harry and Jon to sit beside us. Thomas and Mary Alice snuggled down onto the other side of the table. There was a comfortable silence among the six of us for a few moments before the sound of fireworks popping had us turning our heads skyward to view the spectacle.

It was a night for remembering many things; for thinking back and looking forward; for hope and trust, and more than anything else, for being grateful for the gift of friends, who sometimes appeared in the most unpredictable of circumstances. I glanced up at the sky and said a silent *thank you*. I could almost be certain I heard a clear but faint "*You're welcome, dear girl*" in return.

ANNELL ST. CHARLES

Following a long career in the medical profession, Annell St. Charles turned her attention to writing fiction and producing photography. Her first two novels, "The Things Left Unsaid" and "The Choices We Make", were published in 2016. She also has two books of photography: "Sunrise On Hilton Head Island: Coligny Beach" and "Island Life"; and a book of poetry, "The Clam Shell", also published in 2016. She has been a member of the self-proclaimed "Greater Nashville Book and Wine Club" for around 20 years (who she describes as her toughest critics and greatest friends), and holds a certificate in digital photography from the Shaw Institute. She is an avid walker and can usually be found roaming the streets and beaches around her homes in Nashville, Tennessee and Hilton Head Island with her camera slung over one shoulder while she ponders her next work of fiction. She is married to Constantine Tsinakis, and borrows her friend's "Ebie-like" cats every chance she gets.

THE THINGS LEFT UNSAID